Rick Steves'

ITALIAN
PHRASE BOOK

John Muir Publications
Santa Fe, New Mexico

Thanks to the team of people at *Europe Through the Back Door* who helped make this book possible: Mary Carlson, Dave Hoerlein, Mary Romano, and...

Italian translation: Giulia Fiorini and Alessandra Panieri
Italian proofreading: Manfredo Guerzoni
Phonetics: Risa Laib
Layout: Rich Sorensen
Maps: Dave Hoerlein

Edited by Risa Laib and Rich Sorensen

John Muir Publications, P.O. Box 613, Santa Fe, NM 87504

While every effort has been made to keep the content of this book accurate, the author and publisher accept no responsibility whatsoever for anyone ordering bad pizza or getting messed up in any other way because of the linguistic confidence this phrase book has given them.

JMP travel guidebooks by Rick Steves:

Rick Steves' Best of Italy
Rick Steves' Europe Through the Back Door
Europe 101: History and Art for the Traveler
   (with Gene Openshaw)
Mona Winks: Self-Guided Tours of Europe's Top Museums
   (with Gene Openshaw)
Rick Steves' Best of Europe
Rick Steves' Best of France, Belgium & the Netherlands
   (with Steve Smith)
Rick Steves' Best of Great Britain
Rick Steves' Best of Germany, Austria, & Switzerland
Rick Steves' Best of Scandinavia
Rick Steves' Best of Spain & Portugal
Rick Steves' Best of the Baltics & Russia (with Ian Watson)
Rick Steves' Phrase Books: French, Italian, German,
   French/Italian/German, and Spanish/Portuguese
Asia Through the Back Door (with Bob Effertz)
Kidding Around Seattle

Rick Steves' company, **Europe Through the Back Door,** provides many services for budget European travelers, including a free quarterly newsletter/catalog, budget travel books and accessories, a full selection of European railpasses (with free video and travel advice included), Back Door-style European bus tours, and a user-friendly Travel Resource Center in Edmonds, WA. For more information and a free copy of Rick's newsletter, call or write:

Europe Through the Back Door
120 Fourth Avenue N, Box 2009
Edmonds, WA 98020 USA
Tel: 206/771-8303, Fax: 206/771-0833

Contents

Hi, I'm Rick Steves.

I'm the only mono-lingual speaker I know who's had the nerve to design a series of European phrase books. But that's one of the things that makes them better. You see, after twenty summers of travel through Europe, I've learned first-hand (1) what's essential for communication in another country, and (2) what's not. I've assembled these important words and phrases in a logical, no-frills format, and I've worked with native Europeans and seasoned travelers to give you the simplest, clearest translations possible.

But this book is more than just a pocket translator. The words and phrases have been carefully selected to help you have a smarter, smoother trip in my favorite country without going broke. Italy used to be cheap and chaotic. These days it's neither. It's better organized than ever—and often more expensive than France or Germany. The key to getting more out of every travel dollar is to get closer to the local people, and to rely less on entertainment, restaurants, and hotels that cater only to foreign tourists. This book will not only help you order a meal at a locals-only Venetian restaurant—it'll help you talk to the family that runs the place . . . about their kids, social issues, travel dreams, and favorite flavors of *gelati*. Long after your memories of museums have faded, you'll still treasure the personal encounters you had with your new Italian friends.

A good phrase book should help you enjoy your Italian experience—not just survive it—so I've added a healthy dose of humor. But please use these phrases carefully, in a self-effacing spirit. Remember that one ugly American can undo the goodwill built by dozens of culturally-sensitive ones.

To get the most out of this book, take the time to internalize and put into practice my Italian pronunciation tips. Remember that Italians, more than their European neighbors, are forgiving of your linguistic fumbling. Don't worry too much about memorizing grammatical rules, like which gender a particular noun is—the important thing is to rise above sex . . . and communicate!

This book has an English-Italian dictionary and a nifty menu decoder (to help you figure out what's cooking). You'll also find Italian tongue twisters, gestures, telephone tips, and a handy tear-out "cheat sheet." Tear it out and keep it in your pocket, so you can easily use it to memorize key phrases during idle moments. As you prepare for your trip, you may want to read this year's edition of my *Rick Steves' Best of Italy* guidebook.

Italy can be the most intense, difficult and rewarding destination in Europe. Travelers either love it—or they quickly see the big sights and flee to Switzerland. To me, someone's love of Italy is a sign of a good traveler— thoughtful, confident, and extroverted. If this book helps make that happen, or if you have suggestions for making it better, I'd love to hear from you. Happy travels, and good luck as you hurdle the language barrier!

Rick Steves

Getting Started

User-friendly Italian

...is easy to get the hang of. Some Italian words are so familiar, you'd think they were English. If you can say *pizza, lasagna,* and *spaghetti,* you can speak Italian.

There are a few unusual twists to its pronunciation:

C usually sounds like C in cat.
    But *C* followed by *E* or *I* sounds like CH in chance.
CH sounds like C in cat.
E often sounds like AY in play.
G usually sounds like G in get.
    But *G* followed by *E* or *I* sounds like G in gentle.
GH sounds like G in *spaghetti.*
GLI sounds like LI in million. The G is silent.
GN sounds like GN in *lasagna.*
H is never pronounced.
I sounds like EE in seed.
R is rolled as in *brrravo!*
SC usually sounds like SK in skip.
    But *SC* followed by *E* or *I* sounds like SH in shape.
Z usually sounds like TS in hits, and sometimes like the sound of DZ in kids.

Have you ever noticed that most Italian words end in a vowel? It's *o* if the word is masculine and *a* if it's feminine. So a *bambino* gets blue and a *bambina* gets pink. A man is *generoso* (generous), a woman is *generosa.* A man will say, *"Sono sposato"* (I am married). A woman will say, *"Sono sposata."* In this book, we show gender-bender words like this: *generoso[a]*. If you are speaking of a woman (which includes women speaking about themselves), use the *a* ending. It's always pronounced "ah." If a noun or adjective ends in *e*, such as *cantante* (singer) or *gentile* (kind), the same word applies to either sex.

Adjective endings agree with the noun. It's *cara amica* (a dear female friend) and *caro amico* (a dear male friend). Sometimes the adjective comes after the noun, as in *vino rosso* (red wine).

Plurals are formed by changing the final letter of the noun: *a* becomes *e*, and *o* becomes *i*. So it's one *pizza* and two *pizze*, and one cup of *cappuccino* and two cups of *cappuccini*.

Italians usually pronounce every letter in a word, so *due* (two) is doo-ay. Sometimes two vowels share one syllable. *Piano* sounds like peeah-noh. The "peeah" is one syllable. When one vowel in a pair should be emphasized, it will appear in bold letters: *italiano* is ee-tah-lee**ah**-noh.

The key to Italian inflection is to remember this simple rule: most Italian words have their accent on the second-to-last syllable. To override this rule, Italians sometimes insert an accent: *città* (city) is pronounced chee-**tah**.

Italians are animated. You may think two Italians are arguing when in reality they're agreeing enthusiastically. When they do argue, it's fast and furious! Body language is a very important part of communicating in Italy—especially hand gestures (see Gestures for details).

Watch and imitate. Be confident, and have fun communicating in Italian. The Italians really do want to understand you, and are forgiving of a yankee-fied version of their language.

Here's a quick guide to the phonetics we've used in this book:

ah	like A in father.
ay	like AY in play.
eh	like E in let.
ee	like EE in seed.
ehr	sounds like "air."
g	like G in go.
o	like O in cost.
oh	like O in note.
oo	like OO in too.
or	like OR in core.
ow	like OW in cow.
s	like S in sun.
ts	like TS in hits. It's a small explosive sound. Think of *pizza* (pee-tsah).

Italian Basics

Greeting and meeting Italians:

Good day.	**Buon giorno.**	bwohn **jor**-noh
Good morning.	**Buon giorno.**	bwohn **jor**-noh
Good evening.	**Buona sera.**	**bwoh**-nah **say**-rah
Good night.	**Buona notte.**	**bwoh**-nah **not**-tay
Hi / Bye. (informal)	**Ciao.**	chow
Mr. / Mrs.	**Signor / Signora**	**seen**-yor / seen-**yoh**-rah
Miss	**Signorina**	seen-yoh-**ree**-nah
How are you?	**Come sta?**	**koh**-may stah
Very well, thanks.	**Molto bene, grazie.**	**mohl**-toh **behn**-ay **graht**-seeay
And you?	**E lei?**	ay **leh**ee
My name is...	**Mi chiamo...**	mee kee**ah**-moh
What's your name?	**Come si chiama?**	**koh**-may see kee**ah**-mah
Pleased to meet you.	**Piacere.**	peeah-**chay**-ray
Where are you from?	**Di dove è?**	dee **doh**-vay eh
I am / Are you...?	**Sono / È...?**	**soh**-noh / eh
...on vacation	**...in vacanza**	een vah-**kahnt**-sah
...on business	**...qui per lavoro**	kwee pehr lah-**voh**-roh
See you later.	**A più tardi.**	ah pew **tar**-dee
Goodbye.	**Arrivederci.**	ah-ree-vay-**dehr**-chee
Good luck!	**Buona fortuna!**	**bwoh**-nah for-**too**-nah
Have a good trip!	**Buon viaggio!**	bwohn vee**ah**-joh

Survival phrases

In 800, Charlemagne traveled to Rome and became the Holy Roman Emperor using only these phrases. They are repeated on your tear-out cheat sheet later in this book.

The essentials:

Good day.	**Buon giorno.**	bwohn **jor**-noh
Do you speak English?	**Parla inglese?**	**par**-lah een-**glay**-zay
Yes. / No.	**Si. / No.**	see / noh
I don't speak Italian.	**Non parlo l'italiano.**	nohn **par**-loh lee-tah-lee**ah**-noh
I'm sorry.	**Mi dispiace.**	mee dee-spee**ah**-chay
Please.	**Per favore.**	pehr fah-**voh**-ray
Thank you.	**Grazie.**	**graht**-seeay
It's (not) a problem.	**(Non) c'è problema.**	(nohn) cheh proh-**blay**-mah
It's good.	**Va bene.**	vah **behn**-ay
You are very kind.	**Lei è molto gentile.**	**leh**ee eh **mohl**-toh jayn-**tee**-lay
Goodbye!	**Arrivederci!**	ah-ree-vay-**dehr**-chee

Where?

Where is...?	**Dov'è...?**	doh-**veh**
...a hotel	**...un hotel**	oon oh-**tehl**
...a youth hostel	**...un ostello della gioventù**	oon oh-**stehl**-loh **day**-lah joh-vehn-**too**
...a restaurant	**...un ristorante**	oon ree-stoh-**rahn**-tay

...a supermarket	**...un supermercado**	oon soo-pehr-mehr-**kah**-doh
...a pharmacy	**...una farmacia**	**oo**-nah far-mah-**chee**-ah
...a bank	**...una banca**	**oo**-nah **bahn**-kah
...the train station	**...la stazione**	lah staht-seeoh-nay
...tourist information	**...informazioni per turisti**	een-for-maht-seeoh-nee pehr too-**ree**-stee
...the toilet	**...la toilette**	lah twah-**leht**-tay
men	**uomini, signori**	**woh**-mee-nee, seen-**yoh**-ree
women	**donne, signore**	**don**-nay, seen-**yoh**-ray

How much?

How much is it?	**Quanto costa?**	**kwahn**-toh **kos**-tah
Write it?	**Lo scrive?**	loh **skree**-vay
Cheap(er).	**(Più) economico.**	(pew) ay-koh-**noh**-mee-koh
Cheapest.	**Il più economico.**	eel pew ay-koh-**noh**-mee-koh
Is it free?	**È gratis?**	eh **grah**-tees
Is it included?	**È incluso?**	eh een-**kloo**-zoh
Do you have...?	**Ha...?**	ah
I would like...	**Vorrei....**	vor-**reh**ee
We would like...	**Vorremo...**	vor-**ray**-moh
...this.	**...questo.**	**kway**-stoh
...just a little.	**...un pochino.**	oon poh-**kee**-noh
...more.	**...di più.**	dee pew
...a ticket.	**...un biglietto.**	oon beel-**yay**-toh
...a room.	**...una camera.**	**oo**-nah **kah**-may-rah
...the bill.	**...il conto.**	eel **kohn**-toh

How many?

one	**uno**	**oo**-noh
two	**due**	**doo**-ay
three	**tre**	tray
four	**quattro**	**kwah**-troh
five	**cinque**	**cheeng**-kway
six	**sei**	**seh**ee
seven	**sette**	**seht**-tay
eight	**otto**	ot-toh
nine	**nove**	**nov**-ay
ten	**dieci**	deeay-chee
hundred	**cento**	**chehn**-toh
thousand	**mille**	**mee**-lay

When?

At what time?	**A che ora?**	ah kay **oh**-rah
Just a moment.	**Un momento.**	oon moh-**mayn**-toh
Now.	**Adesso.**	ah-**dehs**-soh
soon / later	**presto / tardi**	**prehs**-toh / **tar**-dee
today / tomorrow	**oggi / domani**	**oh**-jee / doh-**mah**-nee

Be creative! You can combine these survival phrases to say: "Two, please," or "No, thank you," or "I'd like a cheap hotel," or "Cheaper, please?" Please is a magic word in any language. If you want something and you don't know the word for it, just point and say *"Per favore"* (Please). If you know the word for what you want, such as the bill, simply say, *"Il conto, per favore"* (The bill, please).

Struggling with Italian:

Do you speak English?	**Parla inglese?**	**par**-lah een-**glay**-zay
Even a teeny weeny bit?	**Nemmeno un pochino?**	nehm-**may**-noh oon poh-**kee**-noh
Please speak English.	**Parli inglese, per favore.**	**par**-lee een-**glay**-zay pehr fah-**voh**-ray
You speak English well.	**Lei parla l'inglese bene.**	**leh**ee par-lah leen-**glay**-zay **behn**-ay
I don't speak Italian.	**Non parlo l'italiano.**	nohn **par**-loh lee-tah-leeah-noh
I speak a little Italian.	**Parlo un po' d'italiano.**	**par**-loh oon poh dee-tah-leeah-noh
What is this in Italian?	**Come si dice questo in italiano?**	**koh**-may see **dee**-chay **kway**-stoh een ee-tah-leeah-noh
Repeat?	**Ripeta?**	ree-**pay**-tah
Slowly.	**Lentamente.**	layn-tah-**mayn**-tay
Do you understand?	**Capisce?**	kah-**pee**-shay
I understand.	**Capisco.**	kah-**pee**-skoh
I don't understand.	**Non capisco.**	nohn kah-**pee**-skoh
Write it?	**Lo scrive?**	loh **skree**-vay
Who speaks English?	**Chi parla inglese?**	kee **par**-lah een-**glay**-zay

Common questions:

How much?	**Quanto?**	**kwahn**-toh
How many?	**Quanti?**	**kwahn**-tee
How long...?	**Quanto tempo...?**	**kwahn**-toh **tehm**-poh
...is the trip	**...ci vuole il viaggio**	chee **vwah**-lay eel veeah-joh
How far?	**Quanto dista?**	**kwahn**-toh **dee**-stah
How?	**Come?**	**koh**-may
Is it possible?	**È possibile?**	eh poh-**see**-bee-lay
Is it necessary?	**È necessario?**	eh nay-say-**sah**-reeoh
Can you help me?	**Può aiutarmi?**	pwoh ah-yoo-**tar**-mee
What?	**Che cosa?**	kay **koh**-zah
What is that?	**Che cos'è quello?**	kay koh-**zeh kway**-loh
What is better?	**Che cos'è meglio?**	kay koh-**zeh mehl**-yoh
When?	**Quando?**	**kwahn**-doh
What time is it?	**Che ora è?**	kay **oh**-rah eh
At what time?	**A che ora?**	ah kay **oh**-rah
On time?	**Puntuale?**	poon-tooah-lay
Late?	**In ritardo?**	een ree-**tar**-doh
When does this...?	**A che ora...?**	ah kay **oh**-rah
...open	**...aprite**	ah-**pree**-tay
...close	**...chiudete**	keeoo-**day**-tay
Do you have...?	**Ha...?**	ah
Can I / Can we...?	**Posso / Possiamo...?**	**pos**-soh / pos-seeah-moh
...have one	**...averne uno**	ah-**vehr**-nay **oo**-noh

...go free	**...andare senza pagare**	ahn-**dah**-ray **sehn**-sah pah-**gah**-ray
Where is...?	**Dov'è...?**	doh-**veh**
Where are...?	**Dove sono...?**	**doh**-vay **soh**-noh
Where can I find...?	**Dove posso trovare...?**	**doh**-vay **pos**-soh troh-**vah**-ray
Who?	**Chi?**	kee
Why?	**Perchè?**	pehr-**keh**
Why not?	**Perchè no?**	pehr-**keh** noh
Yes or no?	**Si o no?**	see oh noh

To prompt a simple answer, ask, *"Si o no?"* (Yes or no?). To turn a word or sentence into a question, ask it in a questioning tone. *"Va bene"* (It's good) becomes *"Va bene?"* (Is it good?). An easy way to say, "Where is the toilet?" is to ask, *"Toilette?"*

Yin and yang:

cheap / expensive	**economico / caro**	ay-koh-**noh**-mee-koh / **kah**-roh
big / small	**grande / piccolo**	**grahn**-day / **pee**-koh-loh
hot / cold	**caldo / freddo**	**kahl**-doh / **fray**-doh
open / closed	**aperto / chiuso**	ah-**pehr**-toh / kee**oo**-zoh
entrance / exit	**entrata / uscita**	ayn-**trah**-tah / oo-**shee**-tah
arrive / depart	**arrivare / partire**	ah-ree-**vah**-ray / par-**tee**-ray
early / late	**presto / più tardi**	**prehs**-toh / pew **tar**-dee
soon / later	**presto / tardi**	**prehs**-toh / **tar**-dee

fast / slow	**veloce / lento**	vay-**loh**-chay / **lehn**-toh
here / there	**qui / lì**	kwee / lee
near / far	**vicino / lontano**	vee-**chee**-noh / lohn-**tah**-noh
good / bad	**buono / cattivo**	**bwoh**-noh / kah-**tee**-voh
best / worst	**il migliore /** **il peggiore**	eel meel-**yoh**-ray / eel pay-**joh**-ray
a little / lots	**poco / tanto**	**poh**-koh / **tahn**-toh
more / less	**più / meno**	pew / **may**-noh
mine / yours	**mio / suo**	**mee**-oh / **soo**-oh
easy / difficult	**facile / difficile**	**fah**-chee-lay / dee-**fee**-chee-lay
left / right	**sinistra / destra**	see-**nee**-strah / **dehs**-trah
up / down	**su / giú**	soo / joo
young / old	**giovane / anziano**	joh-**vah**-nay / ahnt-see-**ah**-noh
new / old	**nuovo / vecchio**	**nwoh**-voh / **vehk**-eeoh
heavy / light	**pesante / leggero**	pay-**zahn**-tay / lay-**jay**-roh
dark / light	**chiaro / scuro**	kee**ah**-roh / **skoo**-roh
beautiful / ugly	**bello / brutto**	**behl**-loh / **broo**-toh
intelligent / stupid	**intelligente / stupido**	een-tehl-ee-**jayn**-tay / **stoo**-pee-doh
vacant / occupied	**libero / occupato**	**lee**-bay-roh / oh-koo-**pah**-toh
with / without	**con / senza**	kohn / **sehn**-sah

Big little words:

I	**io**	**ee**oh
you (formal)	**Lei**	**leh**ee
you (informal)	**tu**	too
we	**noi**	**noh**ee
he	**lui**	lwee
she	**lei**	**leh**ee
they	**loro**	**loh**-roh
and	**e**	ay
at	**a**	ah
because	**perchè**	pehr-**keh**
but	**ma**	mah
by (via)	**in**	een
for	**per**	pehr
from	**da**	dah
here	**qui**	kwee
in	**in**	een
not	**non**	nohn
now	**adesso**	ah-**dehs**-soh
only	**solo**	**soh**-loh
or	**o**	oh
this / that	**questo / quello**	**kway**-stoh / **kway**-loh
to	**a**	ah
very	**molto**	**mohl**-toh

Italian names for places:

Italy	**Italia**	ee-**tahl**-yah
Venice	**Venezia**	vay-**nayt**-seeah
Florence	**Firenze**	fee-**rehnt**-say
Rome	**Roma**	**roh**-mah
Vatican City	**Città del Vaticano**	cheet-**tah** dayl vah-tee-**kah**-noh
Naples	**Napoli**	**nah**-poh-lee
Italian Riviera	**Riviera Ligure**	reev-**yehr**-rah lee-**goo**-ray
Germany	**Germania**	jehr-**mahn**-yah
Munich	**Monaco di Baviera**	**moh**-nah-koh dee bah-vee**ay**-rah
France	**Francia**	**frahn**-chah
Paris	**Parigi**	pah-**ree**-jee
England	**Inghilterra**	een-geel-**tehr**-rah
Netherlands	**Paesi Bassi**	pah-**ay**-zee **bah**-see
Austria	**Austria**	**ow**-streeah
Switzerland	**Svizzera**	**sveet**-say-rah
Spain	**Spagna**	**spahn**-yah
Greece	**Grecia**	**gray**-chah
Turkey	**Turchia**	**toor**-keeah
Europe	**Europa**	ay-oo-**roh**-pah
Russia	**Russia**	**roo**-seeah
Africa	**Africa**	**ah**-free-kah
United States	**Stati Uniti**	**stah**-tee oo-**nee**-tee
Canada	**Canada**	kah-nah-**dah**
world	**mondo**	**mohn**-doh

Handy Italian expressions:

Prego.	**pray**-goh	Can I help you? / Please. / Thanks. / You're welcome. / All right.
Pronto.	**pron**-toh	Hello. (answering phone) / Ready. (other situations)
Ecco.	**ay**-koh	Here it is.
Dica.	**dee**-kah	Tell me.
Senta.	**sayn**-tah	Listen.
Tutto va bene.	**too**-toh vah **behn**-ay	Everything's fine.
È basta.	eh **bah**-stah	That's enough.
È tutto.	eh **too**-toh	That's all.
la dolce vita	lah **dohl**-chay **vee**-tah	the sweet life
il dolce far niente	eel **dohl**-chay far neee**ehn**-tay	the sweetness of doing nothing
...issimo[a]	...**ee**-see-moh	very ("bravo" means good, "bravissimo" means very good)

Numbers

1	**uno**	**oo**-noh
2	**due**	**doo**-ay
3	**tre**	tray
4	**quattro**	**kwah**-troh
5	**cinque**	**cheeng**-kway
6	**sei**	**se**hee
7	**sette**	**seht**-tay
8	**otto**	**ot**-toh
9	**nove**	**nov**-ay
10	**dieci**	dee**ay**-chee
11	**undici**	**oon**-dee-chee
12	**dodici**	**doh**-dee-chee
13	**tredici**	**tray**-dee-chee
14	**quattordici**	kwah-**tor**-dee-chee
15	**quindici**	**kween**-dee-chee
16	**sedici**	**say**-dee-chee
17	**diciassette**	dee-chahs-**seht**-tay
18	**diciotto**	dee-**choh**-toh
19	**diciannove**	dee-chahn-**nov**-ay
20	**venti**	**vayn**-tee
21	**ventuno**	vayn-**too**-noh
22	**ventidue**	vayn-tee-**doo**-ay
23	**ventitrè**	vayn-tee-**tray**
30	**trenta**	**trayn**-tah
31	**trentuno**	trayn-**too**-noh

40	**quaranta**	kwah-**rahn**-tah
41	**quarantuno**	kwah-rahn-**too**-noh
50	**cinquanta**	cheeng-**kwahn**-tah
60	**sessanta**	say-**sahn**-tah
70	**settanta**	say-**tahn**-tah
80	**ottanta**	ot-**tahn**-tah
90	**novanta**	noh-**vahn**-tah
100	**cento**	**chehn**-toh
101	**centouno**	chehn-toh-**oo**-noh
102	**centodue**	chehn-toh-**doo**-ay
200	**duecento**	doo-ay-**chehn**-toh
1000	**mille**	**mee**-lay
1996	**millenovecento novantasei**	**mee**-lay-nov-ay-**chehn**-toh-noh-vahn-tah-**sehee**
2000	**duemila**	doo-ay-**mee**-lah
10,000	**diecimila**	dee**ay**-chee-**mee**-lah
million	**milione**	mee-lee**oh**-nay
billion	**miliardo**	meel-**yar**-doh
first	**primo**	**pree**-moh
second	**secondo**	say-**kohn**-doh
third	**terzo**	**tehrt**-soh
half	**mezzo**	**mehd**-zoh
100%	**cento per cento**	**chehn**-toh pehr **chehn**-toh
number one	**numero uno**	**noo**-may-roh **oo**-noh

Money

Can you change dollars?	**Può cambiare dollari?**	pwoh kahm-bee**ah**-ray **dol**-lah-ree
What is your exchange rate for dollars...?	**Qual'è il cambio del dollari...?**	kwah-**leh** eel **kahm**-beeoh dayl **dol**-lah-ree
...in traveler's checks	**...per traveler's checks**	pehr "traveler's checks"
What is the commission?	**Quant'è la commissione?**	kwahn-**teh** lah koh-mee-seeoh-nay
Any extra fee?	**C'è un sovrapprezzo?**	cheh oon soh-vrah-**preht**-soh
I would like...	**Vorrei....**	vor-**rehee**
...small bills.	**...banconote di piccolo taglio.**	bahn-koh-**noh**-tay dee **pee**-koh-loh **tahl**-yoh
...large bills.	**...banconote di grosso taglio.**	bahn-koh-**noh**-tay dee **groh**-soh **tahl**-yoh
...coins.	**...monete.**	moh-**nay**-tay
Is this a mistake?	**Questo è un errore?**	**kway**-stoh eh oon eh-**roh**-ray
I'm rich.	**Sono ricco[a].**	**soh**-noh **ree**-koh
I'm poor.	**Sono povero[a].**	**soh**-noh **poh**-vay-roh
I'm broke.	**Sono al verde.**	**soh**-noh ahl **vehr**-day
L. 17,000	**diciassettemila lire**	dee-chahs-seht-tay-**mee**-lah **lee**-ray
L. 500	**cinquecento lire**	cheeng-kway-**chehn**-toh **lee**-ray

Key money words:

bank	**banca**	**bahn**-kah
money	**soldi, denaro**	**sohl**-dee, day-**nah**-roh
change money	**cambiare dei soldi**	kahm-beeah-ray **deh**ee **sohl**-dee
exchange	**cambio**	**kahm**-beeoh
commission	**commissione**	koh-mee-seeoh-nay
traveler's check	**traveler's check**	"traveler's check"
credit card	**carta di credito**	**kar**-tah dee **kray**-dee-toh
cash advance	**prelievo**	pray-leeay-voh
cash machine	**cassa automatica**	**kah**-sah ow-toh-**mah**-tee-kah
cashier	**cassiere**	kah-see**ay**-ray
cash	**contante**	kohn-**tahn**-tay
bills	**banconote**	bahn-koh-**noh**-tay
coins	**monete**	moh-**nay**-tay
receipt	**ricevuta**	ree-chay-**voo**-tah

A *lira* is nearly microscopic—it takes around 1500 *lire* to make a dollar. Italian prices sound huge. You'll often hear the words *mille* (thousand) and *mila* (thousands). You can figure out roughly how many dollars you're talking about by covering up the last three numbers, and subtracting about a third. *Ventimila* = 20,000 lire = around $13. During a transaction, beware of the "slow count"—unscrupulous clerks hope you'll get confused and walk away before you get all of your change. Get familiar with the money, figure out roughly what you'll get back, and just . . . wait. Change money carefully in Italy. Bank fees can be steep.

Time

What time is it?	**Che ore sono?**	kay **oh**-ray **soh**-noh
It's...	**È...**	eh
...8:00.	**...le otto.**	lay **ot**-toh
...16:00.	**...le sedici.**	lay **say**-dee-chee
...4:00 in the afternoon.	**...le quattro del pomeriggio.**	lay **kwah**-troh dayl poh-may-**ree**-joh
...10:30 (in the evening).	**...le dieci e trenta (di sera).**	lay deeay-chee ay **trayn**-tah (dee **say**-rah)
...a quarter past nine.	**...le nove e un quarto.**	lay **nov**-ay ay oon **kwar**-toh
...a quarter to eleven.	**...le undici meno un quarto.**	lay **oon**-dee-chee **may**-noh oon **kwar**-toh
...noon.	**...mezzogiorno.**	mehd-zoh-**jor**-noh
...midnight.	**...mezzanotte.**	mehd-zah-**not**-tay
...sunrise / sunset.	**...alba / tramonto.**	**ahl**-bah / trah-**mohn**-toh
...early / late.	**...presto / tardi.**	**prehs**-toh / **tar**-dee
...on time.	**...puntuale.**	poon-tooah-lay

In Italy, the 24-hour clock (or military time) is used by hotels, for opening/closing hours of stores, and for train, bus, and ferry schedules. Friends use the same "clock" we do. You'd meet a friend at 3:00 in the afternoon (*3:00 del pomeriggio*) to catch a train that leaves at 15:15. The Italian afternoon starts around 1:00, but the evening (*sera*) comes later than ours. The greeting *"Buon giornio"* turns to *"Buona sera"* as the sun sets.

Timely words:

minute	**minuto**	mee-**noo**-toh
hour	**ora**	**oh**-rah
morning	**mattina**	mah-**tee**-nah
afternoon	**pomeriggio**	poh-may-**ree**-joh
evening	**sera**	**say**-rah
night	**notte**	**not**-tay
day	**giorno**	**jor**-noh
today	**oggi**	**oh**-jee
yesterday	**ieri**	**yay**-ree
tomorrow	**domani**	doh-**mah**-nee
tomorrow morning	**domani mattina**	doh-**mah**-nee mah-**tee**-nah
day after tomorrow	**dopodomani**	doh-poh-doh-**mah**-nee
anytime	**a qualsiasi ora**	ah kwahl-seeah-zee **oh**-rah
immediately	**immediatamente**	ee-may-deeah-tah-**mayn**-tay
in one hour	**tra un'ora**	trah oon-**oh**-rah
every hour	**ogni ora**	**ohn**-yee **oh**-rah
every day	**ogni giorno**	**ohn**-yee **jor**-noh
last	**passato**	pah-**sah**-toh
this	**questo**	**kway**-stoh
next	**prossimo**	**pros**-see-moh
May 15	**il quindici di maggio**	eel **kween**-dee-chee dee **mah**-joh

TIME

week	**settimana**	say-tee-**mah**-nah
Monday	**lunedì**	loo-nay-**dee**
Tuesday	**martedì**	mar-tay-**dee**
Wednesday	**mercoledì**	mehr-koh-lay-**dee**
Thursday	**giovedì**	joh-vay-**dee**
Friday	**venerdì**	vay-nehr-**dee**
Saturday	**sabato**	**sah**-bah-toh
Sunday	**domenica**	doh-**may**-nee-kah
month	**mese**	**may**-zay
January	**gennaio**	jay-**nah**-yoh
February	**febbraio**	fay-**brah**-yoh
March	**marzo**	**mart**-soh
April	**aprile**	ah-**pree**-lay
May	**maggio**	**mah**-joh
June	**giugno**	**joon**-yoh
July	**luglio**	**lool**-yoh
August	**agosto**	ah-**goh**-stoh
September	**settembre**	say-**tehm**-bray
October	**ottobre**	oh-**toh**-bray
November	**novembre**	noh-**vehm**-bray
December	**dicembre**	dee-**chehm**-bray
year	**anno**	**ahn**-noh
spring	**primavera**	pree-mah-**vay**-rah
summer	**estate**	ay-**stah**-tay
fall	**autunno**	ow-**too**-noh
winter	**inverno**	een-**vehr**-noh

Italian holidays and happy days:

holiday	**festa**	**fehs**-tah
national holiday	**festa nazionale**	**fehs**-tah naht-seeoh-**nah**-lay
religious holiday	**festa religiosa**	**fehs**-tah ray-lee-**joh**-zah
Easter	**Pasqua**	**pahs**-kwah
Merry Christmas!	**Buon Natale!**	bwohn nah-**tah**-lay
Happy new year!	**Felice anno nuovo!**	fay-**lee**-chay **ahn**-noh nooo**oh**-voh
Happy birthday!	**Buon compleanno!**	bwohn kohm-play-**ahn**-noh

Italians celebrate birthdays with the same "Happy birthday" tune that we use. The Italian words mean "Best wishes to you": *Tanti auguri a te, tanti auguri a te, tanti auguri, caro[a] ___, tanti auguri a te!"*

Holidays which strike during tourist season are April 25th (Liberation Day), May 1st (Labor Day), August 15th (*Ferragosto*, or Ascension of Mary), and November 1st (All Saints Day). In Italy, every saint gets a holiday—these are sprinkled throughout the year and celebrated in local communities with flair.

Transportation

Trains:

Is this the line for...?	**Questa è la fila per...?**	kway-stah eh lah fee-lah pehr
...tickets	**...biglietti**	beel-yay-tee
...reservations	**...prenotazioni**	pray-noh-taht-seeoh-nee
How much is the fare to...?	**Quant'è la tariffa per...?**	kwahn-teh lah tah-ree-fah pehr
A ticket to ___.	**Un biglietto per ___.**	oon beel-yay-toh pehr
When is the next train?	**Quando è il prossimo treno?**	kwahn-doh eh eel pros-see-moh tray-noh
I'd like to leave...	**Vorrei partire...**	vor-rehee par-tee-ray
I'd like to arrive...	**Vorrei arrivare...**	vor-rehee ah-ree-vah-ray
...by ___.	**...per le ___.**	pehr lay
...in the morning.	**...la mattina.**	lah mah-tee-nah
...in the afternoon.	**...il pomeriggio.**	eel poh-may-ree-joh
...in the evening.	**...la sera.**	lah say-rah
Is there a...?	**C'è un...?**	cheh oon
...earlier train	**...treno prima**	tray-noh pree-mah

...later train	...treno più tardi	tray-noh pew tar-dee
...overnight train	...treno notturno	tray-noh noh-toor-noh
...supplement	...supplemento	soo-play-mayn-toh
Is there a discount for...?	Fate sconti per...?	fah-tay skohn-tee pehr
...youths / seniors	...giovani / anziani	joh-vah-nee / ahnt-seeah-nee
Is a reservation required?	Ci vuole la prenotazione?	chee vwoh-lay lah pray-noh-taht-seeoh-nay
I'd like to reserve...	Vorrei prenotare...	vor-rehee pray-noh-tah-ray
...a seat.	...un posto.	oon poh-stoh
...a berth.	...una cuccetta.	oo-nah koo-chay-tah
...a sleeper.	...un posto in vagone letto.	oon poh-stoh een vah-goh-nay leht-toh
Where does (the train) leave from?	Da dove parte?	dah doh-vay par-tay
What track?	Quale binario?	kwah-lay bee-nah-reeoh
On time?	Puntuale?	poon-tooah-lay
Late?	In ritardo?	een ree-tar-doh
When will it arrive?	Quando arriva?	kwahn-doh ah-ree-vah
Is it direct?	È diretto?	eh dee-reht-toh
Must I transfer?	Devo cambiare?	day-voh kahm-beeah-ray
When? / Where?	Quando? / Dove?	kwahn-doh / doh-vay
Which train to...?	Quale treno per....?	kwah-lay tray-noh pehr
Which train car to...?	Quale vagone per....?	kwah-lay vah-goh-nay pehr
Is this (seat) free?	È libero?	eh lee-bay-roh
It's my seat.	È il mio posto.	eh eel mee-oh poh-stoh
Save my place?	Mi tenga il posto?	mee tayn-gah eel poh-stoh

TRANSPORTATION

Where are you going?	**Dove va?**	**doh**-vay vah
I'm going to...	**Vado a...**	**vah**-doh ah
Tell me when to get off?	**Mi dica quando devo scendere?**	mee **dee**-kah **kwahn**-doh **day**-voh **shehn**-day-ray

Ticket talk:

ticket	**biglietto**	beel-**yay**-toh
one way	**andata**	ahn-**dah**-tah
roundtrip	**ritorno**	ree-**tor**-noh
first class	**prima classe**	**pree**-mah **klah**-say
second class	**seconda classe**	say-**kohn**-dah **klah**-say
reduced fare	**tariffa ridotta**	tah-**ree**-fah ree-**doh**-tah
validate	**convalidare**	kohn-vah-lee-**dah**-ray
schedule	**orario**	oh-**rah**-reeoh
departure	**partenza**	par-**tehnt**-sah
direct	**diretto**	dee-**reht**-toh
connection	**coincidenza**	koh-een-chee-**dehnt**-sah
reservation	**prenotazione**	pray-noh-taht-see**oh**-nay
non-smoking	**non fumare**	nohn foo-**mah**-ray
seat	**posto**	**poh**-stoh
seat by...	**posto vicino...**	**poh**-stoh vee-**chee**-noh
...the window	**...al finestrino**	ahl fee-nay-**stree**-noh
...the aisle	**...al corridoio**	ahl kor-ree-**doh**-yoh
berth...	**cuccetta...**	koo-**chay**-tah
...upper	**...di sopra**	dee **soh**-prah
...middle	**...in mezzo**	een **mehd**-zoh
...lower	**...di sotto**	dee **soh**-toh
refund	**rimborso**	reem-**bor**-soh

At the train station:

Italian State Railways	**Ferrovie dello Stato (FS)**	fay-**roh**-veeay **day**-loh **stah**-toh
train station	**stazione**	staht-seeoh-nay
train information	**informazioni sui treni**	een-for-maht-seeoh-nee sooee **tray**-nee
train	**treno**	**tray**-noh
high speed train	**inter-city (IC, EC)**	"inter-city"
arrival	**arrivo**	ah-**ree**-voh
departure	**partenza**	par-**tehnt**-sah
delay	**ritardo**	ree-**tar**-doh
waiting room	**sala di attesa, sala d'aspetto**	**sah**-lah dee ah-**tay**-zah, **sah**-lah dah-**spay**-toh
lockers	**armadietti**	ar-mah-deeay-tee
baggage check room	**sala di controllo, consegna**	**sah**-lah dee kohn-**troh**-loh, kohn-**sayn**-yah
lost and found office	**ufficio oggetti smarriti**	oo-**fee**-choh oh-**jeht**-tee smah-**ree**-tee
tourist information	**informazioni per turisti**	een-for-maht-seeoh-nee pehr too-**ree**-stee
to the trains	**ai treni**	ahee **tray**-nee
track or platform	**binario**	bee-**nah**-reeoh
train car	**vagone**	vah-**goh**-nay
dining car	**carrozza ristorante**	kar-**rot**-sah ree-stoh-**rahn**-tay
sleeper car	**carrozza letto**	kar-**rot**-sah **leht**-toh
conductor	**conduttore**	kohn-doo-**toh**-ray

Major rail lines in Italy

Reading train schedules:

a	to
arrivo	arrival (also abbreviated "a")
da	from
domenica	Sunday
eccetto	except
feriali	weekdays including Saturday
ferma a tutte le stazione	stops at all the stations
festivi	Sundays and holidays
fino	until
giorni	days
giornaliero	daily
in ritardo	late
non ferma a...	doesn't stop in...
ogni	every
partenza	departure (also abbreviated "p")
per	for
sabato	Saturday
solo	only
tutti i giorni	daily
vacanza	holiday
1-5	Monday-Friday
6, 7	Saturday, Sunday

Italian schedules use the 24-hour clock. It's like American time until noon. After that, subtract twelve and add p.m. So 13:00 is 1 p.m., 20:00 is 8 p.m., and 24:00 is midnight. If your train is scheduled to depart at 00:01, it'll leave one minute after midnight.

Italian train stations have wonderful (and fun) new schedule computers. Once you've mastered these (start by punching the "English" button), you'll save lots of time figuring out the right train connections. Italian trains come in five types: the slow milk-run *locale*, the slightly faster *diretto*, the *espresso* which stops only at big stations, the speedy *rapido* (also called *IC* or *EC*), and finally, the *Pendolino*, Italy's new bullet train. If you have a train pass, you won't have to pay the supplement for Italy's fast trains, but you (and everyone else) will need to make a reservation for the *Pendolino*.

Buses and subways:

How do I get to...?	**Come si va a...?**	**koh**-may see vah ah
Which bus to...?	**Quale autobus per....?**	**kwah**-lay **ow**-toh-boos pehr
Does it stop at...?	**Si ferma a...?**	see **fehr**-mah ah
Which metro stop for...?	**A quale stazione scendo per...?**	ah **kway**-lay staht-seeoh-nay **shehn**-doh pehr
Must I transfer?	**Devo cambiare?**	**day**-voh kahm-beeah-ray
How much is a ticket?	**Quanto costa un biglietto?**	**kwahn**-toh **kos**-tah oon beel-**yay**-toh
Where can I buy a ticket?	**Dove posso comprare un biglietto?**	**doh**-vay **pos**-soh kohm-**prah**-ray oon beel-**yay**-toh
Is there a one-day pass?	**C'è un biglietto giornaliero?**	cheh oon beel-**yay**-toh jor-nahl-**yay**-roh

When is the...?	Quando parte...?	kwahn-doh par-tay
...first / next / last	...primo / prossimo / ultimo	pree-moh / pros-see-moh / ool-tee-moh
...bus / subway	...autobus / metropolitana	ow-toh-boos / may-troh-poh-lee-tah-nah
What's the frequency per hour / day?	Quante volte passa all'ora / al giorno?	kwahn-tay vohl-tay pah-sah ahl-loh-rah / ahl jor-noh
I'm going to...	Vado a...	vah-doh ah
Tell me when to get off?	Mi dica quando devo scendere?	mee dee-kah kwahn-doh day-voh shehn-day-ray

Key bus and subway words:

ticket	biglietto	beel-yay-toh
city bus	autobus	ow-toh-boos
long-distance bus	pullman	pool-mahn
bus stop	fermata	fehr-mah-tah
bus station	stazione degli autobus	staht-seeoh-nay dayl-yee ow-toh-boos
subway	metropolitana	may-troh-poh-lee-tah-nah
entrance	entrata	ayn-trah-tah
stop	fermata	fehr-mah-tah
exit	uscita	oo-shee-tah
direct	diretto	dee-reht-toh
connection	coincidenza	koh-een-chee-dehnt-sah
map	cartina	kar-tee-nah

Venice has boats instead of buses. Zip around on *traghetti* (gondola ferries) and *vaporetti* (motorized ferries).

Taxis:

Taxi!	**Taxi!**	**tahk**-see
Can you call a taxi?	**Può chiamare un taxi?**	pwoh kee-ah-**mah**-ray oon **tahk**-see
Where is a taxi stand?	**Dov'è una fermata dei taxi?**	doh-**veh oo**-nah fehr-**mah**-tah **deh**ee **tahk**-see
Are you free?	**È libero?**	eh **lee**-bay-roh
Occupied.	**Occupato.**	oh-koo-**pah**-toh
How much is it...?	**Quanto costa...?**	**kwahn**-toh **kos**-tah
...to the airport	**...all'aereoporto**	ah-lah-ay-ray-oh-**por**-toh
...to the train station	**...alla stazione ferroviaria**	**ah**-lah staht-see**oh**-nay fay-roh-vee-**ah**-reeah
...to this address	**...a questo indirizzo**	ah **kway**-stoh een-dee-**reet**-soh
Too much.	**Troppo.**	**trop**-poh
This is all I have.	**Questo è tutto quel che ho.**	**kway**-stoh eh **too**-toh kwayl kay oh
Can you take ___ people?	**Può portar ___ persone?**	pwoh **por**-tar ___ pehr-**soh**-nay
Any extra fee?	**C'è un sovrapprezzo?**	cheh oon soh-vrah-**preht**-soh
The meter, please.	**Il tassametro, per favore.**	eel tah-sah-**may**-troh pehr fah-**voh**-ray
The most direct route.	**Il percorso più breve.**	eel pehr-**kor**-soh pew **bray**-vay
Slow down.	**Rallenti.**	rah-**lehn**-tee
If you don't slow down, I'll throw up.	**Se non rallenta, vomito.**	say nohn rah-**lehn**-tah, **voh**-mee-toh

Stop here.	**Si fermi qui.**	see **fehr**-mee kwee
Can you wait?	**Può aspettare?**	pwoh ah-spay-**tah**-ray
I'll never forget this ride.	**Non dimenticherò mai questo viaggio.**	nohn dee-mayn-tee-kay-**roh mahee kway**-stoh veeah-joh
Where did you learn to drive?	**Ma dove ha imparato a guidare?**	mah **doh**-vay ah eem-pah-**rah**-toh ah gwee-**dah**-ray
I'll only pay what's on the meter.	**Pago solo la cifra sul tassametro.**	**pah**-goh **soh**-loh lah **chee**-frah sool tah-sah-**may**-troh
My change, please.	**Il resto, per favore.**	eel **rehs**-toh pehr fah-**voh**-ray
Keep the change.	**Tenga il resto.**	**tayn**-gah eel **rehs**-toh

Tipping is not necessary, but if you've had a particularly helpful driver, round up to the nearest thousand *lire* (and add a thousand if you wish). Cab fares are reasonable and most drivers are honest. Three or more tourists are usually better off hailing a cab than messing with city buses in Italy. If cabs won't stop for you, your luck may improve at a nearby *fermata dei taxi* (taxi stand).

TRANSPORTATION

Rental wheels:

I'd like to rent...	**Vorrei affittare...**	vor-**reh**ee ah-feet-**tah**-ray
...a car.	**...una macchina.**	**oo**-nah **mah**-kee-nah
...a station wagon.	**...una station wagon.**	**oo**-nah **staht**-see-ohn **wah**-gohn
...a van.	**...un pulmino.**	oon pool-**mee**-noh
...a motorcycle.	**...una motocicletta.**	**oo**-nah moh-toh-chee-**klay**-tah
...a motor scooter.	**...un motorino.**	oon moh-toh-**ree**-noh
...a bicycle.	**...una bicicletta.**	**oo**-nah bee-chee-**klay**-tah
How much...?	**Quanto...?**	**kwahn**-toh
...per hour	**...all'ora**	ah-**loh**-rah
...per day	**...al giorno**	ahl **jor**-noh
...per week	**...alla settimana**	**ah**-lah say-tee-**mah**-nah
Unlimited mileage?	**Chilometraggio illimitato?**	kee-loh-may-**trah**-joh eel-lee-mee-**tah**-toh
I brake for bakeries.	**Mi fermo ad ogni pasticceria.**	mee **fehr**-moh ahd **ohn**-yee pah-stee-chay-**ree**-ah
Is there...?	**C'è...?**	cheh
...a helmet	**...un casco**	oon **kah**-skoh
...a discount	**...uno sconto**	**oo**-noh **skohn**-toh
...a deposit	**...un deposito**	oon day-**poh**-zee-toh
...insurance	**...l'assicurazione**	lah-see-koo-raht-see**oh**-nay
When do I bring it back?	**Quando lo riporto indietro?**	**kwahn**-doh loh ree-**por**-toh een-dee**ay**-troh

Driving:

gas station	**benzinaio**	baynd-zee-**nah**-yoh
The nearest gas station?	**Il benzinaio più vicino?**	eel baynd-zee-**nah**-yoh pew vee-**chee**-noh
Self-service?	**Self-service?**	"self service"
Fill the tank.	**Il pieno.**	eel peeay-noh
I need...	**Ho bisogno di...**	oh bee-**zohn**-yoh dee
...gas.	**...benzina.**	baynd-**zee**-nah
...unleaded.	**...benzina verde.**	baynd-**zee**-nah **vehr**-day
...regular.	**...normale.**	nor-**mah**-lay
...super.	**...super.**	**soo**-pehr
...diesel.	**...gasolio.**	gah-**zoh**-leeoh
Check...	**Controlli...**	kohn-**troh**-lee
...the oil.	**...l'olio.**	**loh**-leeoh
...the tires.	**...le gomme.**	lay **goh**-may
...the radiator.	**...il radiatore.**	eel rah-deeah-**toh**-ray
...the battery.	**...la batteria.**	lah bah-tay-**ree**-ah
...the fuses.	**...i fusibili.**	ee foo-**zee**-bee-lee
...the fanbelt.	**...la cinghia del ventilatore.**	lah **cheen**-geeah dayl vehn-tee-lah-**toh**-ray
...the brakes.	**...i freni,**	ee **fray**-nee
...my pulse.	**...il mio battito cardiaco.**	eel **mee**-oh bah-**tee**-toh kar-deeah-koh

Filling up the tank in Italy is just like at home, except the pump says *lire* and liters rather than dollars and gallons.

The freeway rest stops and city *automat* gas pumps are the only places that sell gas during the afternoon siesta hours. Gas is always more expensive on the super highways. Italy's famous coupons for cheaper gas (available only to tourists at the border crossings) are not worth the complexity they add to your travels.

Car trouble:

accident	**incidente**	een-chee-**dehn**-tay
breakdown	**guasto**	gooah-stoh
funny noise	**rumore strano**	roo-**moh**-ray **strah**-noh
electrical problem	**problema elettrico**	proh-**blay**-mah ay-**leht**-ree-koh
flat tire	**gomma a terra**	**goh**-mah ah **tay**-rah
My car won't start.	**La mia macchina non parte.**	lah **mee**-ah **mah**-kee-nah nohn **par**-tay
This doesn't work.	**Non funziona.**	nohn foont-seeoh-nah
It's overheating.	**Si sta surriscaldando.**	see stah soo-ree-skahl-**dahn**-doh
I need...	**Ho bisogno di...**	oh bee-**zohn**-yoh dee
...a tow truck.	**...un carro attrezzi.**	oon **kar**-roh ah-**trayt**-see
...a mechanic.	**...un meccanico.**	oon may-**kah**-nee-koh
...a stiff drink.	**...whiskey.**	"whiskey"

For help with repair, look up "Repair" under Shopping.

Parking:

parking garage	**garage**	gah-**rahj**
Where can I park?	**Dove posso parcheggiare?**	**doh**-vay **pos**-soh par-kay-**jah**-ray
Is parking nearby?	**È vicino il parcheggio?**	eh vee-**chee**-noh eel par-**kay**-joh
Can I park here?	**Posso parcheggiare qui?**	**pos**-soh par-kay-**jah**-ray kwee
How long can I park here?	**Per quanto tempo posso parcheggiare qui?**	pehr **kwahn**-toh **tehm**-poh **pos**-soh par-kay-**jah**-ray kwee
Must I pay to park here?	**È a pagamento questo parcheggio?**	eh ah pah-gah-**mayn**-toh **kway**-stoh par-**kay**-joh
Is this a safe place to park?	**È sicuro parcheggiare qui?**	eh see-**koo**-roh par-kay-**jah**-ray kwee

Parking in Italian cities is expensive and hazardous. Plan to pay to use a parking garage in big cities. Leave nothing in your car at night. Always ask at your hotel about safe parking. Take parking restrictions seriously to avoid getting fines and having your car towed away (an interesting but costly experience).

Finding your way:

I am going to...	**Vado a...**	**vah**-doh ah
How do I get to...?	**Come si va a...?**	**koh**-may see vah ah
Is there a map?	**C'e una cartina?**	cheh **oo**-nah kar-**tee**-nah
How many minutes...?	**Quanti minuti...?**	**kwahn**-tee mee-**noo**-tee
How many hours...?	**Quante ore...?**	**kwahn**-tay **oh**-ray
...on foot	**...a piedi**	ah pee**ay**-dee
...by bicycle	**...in bicicletta**	een bee-chee-**klay**-tah
...by car	**...in macchina**	een **mah**-kee-nah
How many kilometers to...?	**Quanti chilometri per...?**	**kwahn**-tee kee-**loh**-may-tree pehr
What is the... route to Rome?	**Qual'è la strada... per andare a Roma?**	kwah-**leh** lah **strah**-dah... pehr ahn-**dah**-ray ah **roh**-mah
...best	**...migliore**	meel-**yoh**-ray
...fastest	**...più veloce**	pew vay-**loh**-chay
...most interesting	**...più interessante**	pew een-tay-ray-**sahn**-tay
Point it out?	**Me lo mostri?**	may loh **mohs**-tree
I'm lost.	**Mi sono perso[a].**	mee **soh**-noh **pehr**-soh
Where am I?	**Dove sono?**	**doh**-vay **soh**-noh
Who am I?	**Chi sono?**	kee **soh**-noh
Where is...?	**Dov'è...?**	doh-**veh**
The nearest...?	**Il più vicino...?**	eel pew vee-**chee**-noh
Where is this address?	**Dov'è questo indirizzo?**	doh-**veh kway**-stoh een-dee-**reet**-soh

In Italy, the shortest distance between any two points is
the *autostrada*, though the tolls are not cheap (about a
dollar for each ten minutes). There are not as many signs
as we are used to, so stay alert or you may miss your exit!
Italy's *autostrada* rest stops are among the best in Europe.

Key route-finding words:

map	**cartina**	kar-**tee**-nah
road map	**cartina stradale**	kar-**tee**-nah strah-**dah**-lay
straight ahead	**sempre diritto**	**sehm**-pray dee-**ree**-toh
left / right	**sinistra / destra**	see-**nee**-strah / **dehs**-trah
first / next	**prima / prossima**	**pree**-mah / **pros**-see-mah
intersection	**intersezione**	een-tehr-seht-see**oh**-nay
stoplight	**semaforo**	say-mah-**foh**-roh
(main) square	**piazza (principale)**	pee**aht**-sah (preen-chee-**pah**-lay)
street	**strada, via**	**strah**-dah, **vee**-ah
bridge	**ponte**	**pohn**-tay
tunnel	**tunnel**	**toon**-nel
highway	**autostrada**	ow-toh-**strah**-dah
freeway	**superstrada**	soo-pehr-**strah**-dah
north / south	**nord / sud**	nord / sood
east / west	**est / ovest**	ayst / **oh**-vehst

As in any country, the flashing lights of a patrol car are a sure sign that someone's in trouble. If it's you, say: *"Mi dispiace, sono un turista."* (Sorry, I'm a tourist.) Or, for an unforgettable experience, say: *"Se non le piace come guido, si tolga dal marciapiede."* (If you don't like how I drive, stay off the sidewalk.)

Reading road signs:

alt / stop	stop
carabinieri	police
centro città	to the center of town
circonvallazione	ring road
dare la precedenza	yield
deviazione	detour
entrata	entrance
lavori in corso	road work ahead
rallentare	slow down
senso unico	one-way street
tutte le (altre) destinazioni	to all (other) destinations
uscita	exit
zona pedonale	pedestrian zone

Here are the standard symbols you'll see:

DUH   NO ENTRY FOR CARS   ALL VEHICLES PROHIBITED   NO ENTRY   SPEED LIMIT (IN KM)   YIELD   NO PASSING   DANGER   PARKING

Other signs you may bump into:

acqua non potabile	undrinkable water
affittasi, in affitto	for rent or for hire
aperto	open
aperto da... a...	open from... to...
attenzione	caution
bagno / gabinetto / toilette / toletta / WC	toilet
camare libere	vacancy
chiuso	closed
chiuso per ferie	closed for vacation
chiuso per restauro	closed for restoration
completo	no vacancy
donne	women
entrata libera	free admission
entrata vietata	no entry
fuori de servizio / guasto	out of service
non toccare	do not touch
occupato	occupied
parcheggio vietato	no parking
pericolo	danger
sciopero	on strike
signore	women
signori	men
saldo	sale
uomini	men
uscita d'emergenza	emergency exit
vendesi, in vendita	for sale
vietato	forbidden
vietato fumare	no smoking
vietato l'accesso	keep out

TRANSPORTATION

Sleeping

Places to stay:

hotel	**hotel, albergo**	**oh**-tehl, ahl-**behr**-goh
small hotel (usually family-run)	**pensione, locanda**	payn-seeoh-nay, loh-**kahn**-dah
room in private home	**camera in affitto**	**kah**-may-rah een ah-**fee**-toh
youth hostel	**ostello della gioventù**	oh-**stehl**-loh **day**-lah joh-vehn-**too**
vacancy	**camere libere**	**kah**-may-rah **lee**-bay-ray
no vacancy	**completo**	kohm-**play**-toh

Reserving a room:

Impress your friends by reserving a room by phone. A good time to call is the morning of the day you plan to arrive. If you want to reserve by fax, use the nifty form on the last page of this book.

Hello.	**Buon giorno.**	bwohn **jor**-noh
Do you speak English?	**Parla inglese?**	**par**-lah een-**glay**-zay
Do you have a room...?	**Avete una camera...?**	ah-**vay**-tay **oo**-nah **kah**-may-rah
...for one person / two people	**...per una persona / due persone**	pehr **oo**-nah pehr-**soh**-nah / **doo**-ay pehr-**soh**-nay
...for tonight	**...per stanotte**	pehr stah-**not**-tay
...for two nights	**...per due notti**	pehr **doo**-ay **not**-tee

...for this Friday	**...per venerdì**	pehr vay-nehr-**dee**
...for June 21	**...per ventuno giugno**	pehr vayn-**too**-noh **joon**-yoh
Yes or no?	**Sì o no?**	see oh noh
I'd like...	**Vorrei...**	vor-**reh**ee
...a private bathroom.	**...un bagno completo.**	oon **bahn**-yoh kohm-**play**-toh
...your cheapest room.	**...la camera più economico.**	lah **kah**-may-rah pew ay-koh-**noh**-mee-koh
...___ bed (beds)	**...___ letto (letti)**	___ **leht**-toh (**leht**-tee)
for ___ people	**per ___ persone**	pehr ___ pehr-**soh**-nay
in ___ room (rooms).	**nella ___ camera (camere).**	**nay**-lah ___ **kah**-may-rah (**kah**-may-ray)
How much is it?	**Quanto costa?**	**kwahn**-toh **kos**-tah
Anything cheaper?	**Niente di più economico?**	nee-**ehn**-tay dee pew ay-koh-**noh**-mee-koh
I'll take it.	**La prendo.**	lah **prehn**-doh
My name is...	**Mi chiamo...**	mee keeah-moh
I'll stay / We'll stay...	**Starò / Staremo...**	stah-**roh** / stah-**ray**-moh
...for ___ night (nights).	**...per ___ notte (notti).**	pehr ___ **not**-tay (**not**-tee)
I'll come / We'll come...	**Arriverò / Arriveremo...**	ah-ree-vay-**roh** / ah-ree-vay-**ray**-moh
...in one hour.	**...tra un'ora.**	trah oon-**oh**-rah
...before 16:00.	**...prima delle sedici.**	**pree**-mah **day**-lay **say**-dee-chee
...Friday before 6 p.m.	**...venerdí prima le sei di sera.**	vay-nehr-**dee pree**-mah lay seh ee dee **say**-rah
Thank you.	**Grazie.**	**graht**-seeay

SLEEPING

Getting specific:

I'd like a room...	**Vorrei una camera...**	vor-**rehee** oo-nah **kah**-may-rah
...with / without / and	**...con / senza / e**	kohn / **sehn**-sah / ay
...toilet	**...toilette**	twah-**leht**-tay
...shower	**...doccia**	**doh**-chah
...shower down the hall	**...doccia in fondo al corridoio**	**doh**-chah een **fohn**-doh ahl kor-ree-**doh**-yoh
...bathtub	**...vasca da bagno**	**vah**-skah dah **bahn**-yoh
...double bed	**...letto matrimoniale**	**leht**-toh mah-tree-moh-neeah-lay
...twin beds	**...letti singoli**	**leht**-tee **seeng**-goh-lee
...balcony	**...balcone**	bahl-**koh**-nay
...view	**...vista**	**vee**-stah
...only a sink	**...solo un lavandino**	**soh**-loh oon lah-vahn-**dee**-noh
...on the ground floor	**...al piano terreno**	ahl peeah-noh tay-**ray**-noh
Is there an elevator?	**Un ascensore?**	oon ah-shayn-**soh**-ray
We arrive Monday, depart Wednesday.	**Arriviamo lunedì, ripartiamo mercoledì.**	ah-ree-veeah-moh loo-nay-dee, ree-par-teeah-moh mehr-koh-lay-**dee**
I have a reservation.	**Ho una prenotazione.**	oh oo-nah pray-noh-taht-see**oh**-nay
Confirm my reservation?	**Confermi la mia prenotazione?**	kohn-**fehr**-mee lah **mee**-ah pray-noh-taht-see**oh**-nay

I'll sleep anywhere.	**Posso dormire**	**pos**-soh dor-**mee**-ray
I'm desperate.	**ovunque. Sono**	oh-**voon**-kway. **soh**-noh
	disperato[a].	dee-spay-**rah**-toh
I have a sleeping bag.	**Ho un sacco a pelo.**	oh oon **sah**-koh ah **pay**-loh

Nailing down the price:

How much is...?	**Quanto costa...?**	**kwahn**-toh **kos**-tah
...a room for ___ people	**...una camera per ___ persone**	oo-nah **kah**-may-rah pehr ___ pehr-**soh**-nay
...your cheapest room	**...la camera più economica**	lah **kah**-may-rah pew ay-koh-**noh**-mee-kah
Is breakfast included?	**La colazione è inclusa?**	lah koh-laht-seeoh-nay eh een-**kloo**-zah
Is breakfast required?	**È obbligatoria la colazione?**	eh oh-blee-gah-**toh**-reeah lah koh-laht-seeoh-nay
How much without breakfast?	**Quant'è senza la colazione?**	kwahn-**teh sehn**-sah lah koh-laht-seeoh-nay
Complete price?	**Prezzo completo?**	**preht**-soh kohm-**play**-toh
Is it cheaper if I stay ___ nights?	**È più economico se mi fermo ___ notti?**	eh pew ay-koh-**noh**-mee-koh say mee **fehr**-moh ___ **not**-tee
I will stay ___ nights.	**Mi fermo ___ notti.**	mee **fehr**-moh ___ **not**-tee

Italian hotels almost always have larger rooms to fit three to six people. Your price per person plummets as you pack more into a room. Breakfasts are usually basic (coffee, rolls and marmalade) and expensive ($6 to $8). They're often optional.

Choosing a room:

Can I see the room?	**Posso vedere la camera?**	**pos**-soh vay-**day**-ray lah **kah**-may-rah
Show me another room?	**Mi mostri un'altra camera?**	mee **moh**-stree oo-**nahl**-trah **kah**-may-rah
Do you have something...?	**Avete qualcosa...?**	ah-**vay**-tay kwahl-**koh**-zah
...larger / smaller	**...di più grande / di più piccolo**	dee pew **grahn**-day / dee pew **pee**-koh-loh
...better / cheaper	**...di meglio / più economico**	dee **mehl**-yoh / pew ay-koh-**noh**-mee-koh
...brighter	**...più luminoso**	pew loo-mee-**noh**-zoh
...in the back	**...nella parte di dietro**	**nay**-lah **par**-tay dee **deeay**-troh
...quieter	**...di più tranquillo**	dee pew trahn-**kwee**-loh
I'll take it.	**La prendo.**	lah **prehn**-doh
My key, please.	**La mia chiave, per favore.**	lah **mee**-ah keeah-vay pehr fah-**voh**-ray
Sleep well.	**Sogni d'oro.**	**sohn**-yee **doh**-roh
Good night.	**Buona notte.**	**bwoh**-nah **not**-tay

Hotel help:

I'd like...	**Vorrei...**	vor-**rehee**
...a / another	**...un / un altro**	oon / oon **ahl**-troh
...towel.	**...asciugamano.**	ah-shoo-gah-**mah**-noh
...pillow.	**...cuscino.**	koo-**shee**-noh

...clean sheets.	...lenzuola pulite.	lehnt-soooh-lah poo-lee-tay
...blanket.	...coperta.	koh-pehr-tah
...glass.	...bicchiere.	bee-keeay-ray
...sink stopper.	...tappo.	tah-poh
...soap.	...sapone.	sah-poh-nay
...toilet paper.	...carta igienica.	kar-tah ee-jay-nee-kah
...crib.	...culla.	koo-lah
...small extra bed.	...extra letto singolo.	ehk-strah leht-toh seeng-goh-loh
...different room.	...altra camera.	ahl-trah kah-may-rah
...silence.	...silenzio.	see-lehnt-seeoh
Where can I... my laundry?	Dove posso... bucato?	doh-vay pos-soh... boo-kah-toh
...wash	...fare del	fah-ray dayl
...hang	...stendere il	stehn-day-ray eel
I'd like to stay another night.	Vorrei fermarmi un'altra notte.	vor-rehee fehr-mar-mee oo-nahl-trah not-tay
Where can I park?	Dove posso parcheggiare?	doh-vay pos-soh par-kay-jah-ray
When do you lock up?	A che ora chiude?	ah kay oh-rah keeoo-day
What time is breakfast?	A che ora è la colazione?	ah kay oh-rah eh lah koh-laht-seeoh-nay
Please wake me at 7:00.	Mi svegli alle sette, per favore.	mee zvayl-yee ah-lay seht-tay pehr fah-voh-ray

SLEEPING

Hotel hassles:

Come with me.	**Venga con me.**	**vayn**-gah kohn may
I have a problem in my room.	**Ho un problema con la mia camera.**	oh oon proh-**blay**-mah kohn lah **mee**-ah **kah**-may-rah
bad odor	**cattivo odore**	kah-**tee**-voh oh-**doh**-ray
bugs	**insetti**	een-**seht**-tee
mice	**topi**	**top**-ee
prostitutes	**prostitute**	proh-stee-**too**-tay
The bed is too soft / hard.	**Il letto è troppo morbido / duro.**	eel **leht**-toh eh **trop**-poh **mor**-bee-doh / **doo**-roh
I'm covered with bug bites.	**Sono pieno[a] di punture di insetti.**	**soh**-noh peeay-noh dee poon-**too**-ray dee een-**seht**-tee
Lamp...	**Lampada...**	lahm-**pah**-dah
Lightbulb...	**Lampadina...**	lahm-pah-**dee**-nah
Key...	**Chiave...**	keeah-vay
Lock...	**Serratura...**	say-rah-**too**-rah
Window...	**Finestra...**	fee-**nay**-strah
Faucet...	**Rubinetto...**	roo-bee-**nay**-toh
Sink...	**Lavabo...**	**lah**-vah-boh
Toilet...	**Toilette...**	twah-**leht**-tay
Shower...	**Doccia...**	**doh**-chah
...doesn't work.	**...non funziona.**	nohn foont-seeoh-nah
There is no hot water.	**Non c'è acqua calda.**	nohn cheh **ah**-kwah **kahl**-dah

| When is the water hot? | **A che ora è calda l'acqua?** | ah kay **oh**-rah eh **kahl**-dah **lah**-kwah |

Checking out:

I'll leave / We'll leave...	**Parto / Partiamo...**	**par**-toh / par-tee**ah**-moh
...today / tomorrow.	**...oggi / domani.**	**oh**-jee / doh-**mah**-nee
...very early.	**...molto presto.**	**mohl**-toh **prehs**-toh
When is check-out time?	**A che ora devo lasciare la camera?**	ah kay **oh**-rah **day**-voh lah-**shah**-ray lah **kah**-may-rah
Can I pay now?	**Posso pagare subito?**	**pos**-soh pah-**gah**-ray **soo**-bee-toh
The bill, please.	**Il conto, per favore.**	eel **kohn**-toh pehr fah-**voh**-ray
Credit card O.K.?	**Carta di credito è O.K.?**	**kar**-tah dee **kray**-dee-toh eh "O.K."
I slept like a rock.	**Ho dormito come un sasso.**	oh dor-**mee**-toh **koh**-may oon **sah**-soh
Everything was great.	**Tutto magnifico.**	**too**-toh mahn-**yee**-fee-koh
Will you call my next hotel for me?	**Può telefonare a questo altro albergo per me?**	pwoh tay-lay-foh-**nah**-ray ah **kway**-stoh **ahl**-troh ahl-**behr**-goh pehr may
Can I / Can we...?	**Posso / Possiamo...?**	**pos**-soh / pos-see**ah**-moh
...leave baggage here until ___	**...lasciare il bagaglio qui fino a ___**	lah-**shah**-ray eel bah-**gahl**-yoh kwee **fee**-noh ah

SLEEPING

Camping:

tent	**tenda**	**tayn**-dah
camping	**campeggio**	kahm-**pay**-joh
Where is the nearest campground?	**Dov'è il campeggio più vicino?**	doh-**veh** eel kahm-**pay**-joh pew vee-**chee**-noh
Can I / Can we...?	**Posso / Possiamo...?**	**pos**-soh / pos-seeah-moh
...camp here for the night	**...campeggiare qui per la notte**	kahm-pay-**jah**-ray kwee pehr lah **not**-tay
Do showers cost extra?	**Costano extra le docce?**	koh-**stah**-noh **ehk**-strah lay **doh**-chay
shower token	**gettone**	jay-**toh**-nay

In some Italian campgrounds and youth hostels, you must buy a *gettone* (token) to activate a coin-operated hot shower. It has a timer inside, like a parking meter. To avoid a sudden cold rinse, buy at least two *gettoni* before getting undressed.

Eating

Finding a restaurant:

Where's a good... restaurant?	**Dov'è un buon ristorante...?**	doh-**veh** oon bwohn ree-stoh-**rahn**-tay
...cheap	**...economico**	ay-koh-**noh**-mee-koh
...local-style	**...con cucina casereccia**	kohn koo-**chee**-nah kah-zay-**ray**-chah
...untouristy	**...non per turisti**	nohn pehr too-**ree**-stee
...Chinese	**...cinese**	chee-**nay**-zay
...fast food (Italian-style)	**...tavola calda**	**tah**-voh-lah **kahl**-dah
...cafeteria	**...self-service**	"self-service"
...with a salad bar	**...con un banco delle insalate**	kohn oon **bahn**-koh **day**-lay een-sah-**lah**-tay

Getting a table and menu:

Waiter.	**Cameriere.**	kah-may-reeay-ray
Waitress.	**Cameriera.**	kah-may-reeay-rah
I'd like...	**Vorrei...**	vor-**reh**ee
...a table for one / two.	**...un tavolo per uno[a] / due.**	oon **tah**-voh-loh pehr **oo**-noh / **doo**-ay
...non-smoking.	**...non fumatori.**	nohn foo-mah-**toh**-ree
...just a drink.	**...soltanto qualcosa da bere.**	sohl-**tahn**-toh kwahl-**koh**-zah dah **bay**-ray
...a snack.	**...un spuntino.**	oon spoon-**tee**-noh
...only a pasta dish.	**...solo un primo piatto.**	**soh**-loh oon **pree**-moh peeah-toh
...to see the menu.	**...vedere il menù.**	vay-**day**-ray eel may-**noo**

...to order.	...ordinare.	or-dee-**nah**-ray
...to eat.	...mangiare.	mahn-**jah**-ray
...to pay.	...pagare.	pah-**gah**-ray
...to throw up.	...vomitare.	voh-mee-**tah**-ray
What do you recommend?	**Che cosa raccomanda?**	kay **koh**-zah rah-koh-**mahn**-dah
What's your favorite?	**Qual'è il suo preferito?**	kwah-**leh** eel **soo**-oh pray-fay-**ree**-toh
Is it ...?	**È...?**	eh
...good	...**buono**	**bwoh**-noh
...expensive	...**caro**	**kah**-roh
...light	...**leggero**	lay-**jay**-roh
...filling	...**sostanzioso**	soh-stahnt-see**oh**-zoh
What is...?	**Che cosa c'è...?**	kay **koh**-zah cheh
...that	...**quello**	**kway**-loh
...local	...**di locale**	dee loh-**kah**-lay
...fast	...**di veloce**	dee vay-**loh**-chay
...cheap and filling	...**di economico e sostanzioso**	dee ay-koh-**noh**-mee-koh ay soh-stahnt-see**oh**-zoh
Do you have...?	**Avete...?**	ah-**vay**-tay
...an English menu	...**un menù in inglese**	oon may-**noo** een een-**glay**-zay
...children's portions	...**le porzioni per bambini**	lay port-see**oh**-nee pehr bahm-**bee**-nee

The menu:

menu	**menù**	may-**noo**
menu of the day	**menù del giorno**	may-**noo** dayl **jor**-noh
tourist menu	**menù turistico**	may-**noo** too-**ree**-stee-koh
specialty of the house	**specialità della casa**	spay-chah-lee-**tah day**-lah **kah**-zah
chef's speciality	**capricciosa**	kah-pree-**choh**-zah
breakfast	**colazione**	koh-laht-seeoh-nay
lunch	**pranzo**	**prahnt**-soh
dinner	**cena**	**chay**-nah
appetizers	**antipasti**	ahn-tee-**pah**-stee
bread	**pane**	**pah**-nay
salad	**insalata**	een-sah-**lah**-tah
soup	**minestra, zuppa**	mee-**nehs**-trah, **tsoo**-pah
first course (pasta, soup)	**primo piatto**	**pree**-moh peeah-toh
main course (meat, fish)	**secondo piatto**	say-**kohn**-doh peeah-toh
meat	**carni**	**kar**-nee
poultry	**pollame**	poh-**lah**-may
seafood	**frutti di mare**	**froo**-tee dee **mah**-ray
side dishes	**contorni**	kohn-**tor**-nee
vegetables	**legumi**	lay-**goo**-mee
cheeses	**formaggi**	for-**mah**-jee
desserts	**dolci**	**dohl**-chee
beverages	**bevande, bibite**	bay-**vahn**-day, **bee**-bee-tay

beer	**birra**	**beer**-rah
wines	**vini**	**vee**-nee
cover charge	**coperto**	koh-**pehr**-toh
service (not) included	**servizio (non) incluso**	sehr-**veet**-seeoh (nohn) een-**kloo**-zoh
with / and /	**con / e /**	kohn / ay /
or / without	**o / senza**	oh / **sehn**-sah

EATING

Pay attention to the money-saving words in this chapter. Without them, Italy is a very expensive place to eat. Most menus explain the *servizio* (service) charge which will be added to your bill along with the *coperto* (cover charge).

Budget eaters do best in places with no or minimal service and cover charges, and by sticking to the *primo piatto* (first course dishes). A hearty *minestrone* and/or *pasta* fills the average American. Pricier restaurants are wise to this, and some don't allow you to eat without ordering the expensive *secondo* course.

Often a good deal, a *menù del giorno* (menu of the day) offers you a choice of appetizer, entrée, and dessert (or wine) at a fixed price.

Dietary restrictions:

I'm allergic to...	**Sono allergico[a] al...**	**soh**-noh ahl-**lehr**-jee-koh ahl
I cannot eat...	**Non posso mangiare...**	nohn **pos**-soh mahn-**jah**-ray
...dairy products.	**...prodotti casearei.**	proh-**dot**-tee kah-zay-ah-**ray**ee
...meat / pork.	**...carne / maiale.**	**car**-nay / mah-**yah**-lay
...salt / sugar.	**...sale / zucchero.**	**sah**-lay / **tsoo**-kay-roh
I am diabetic.	**Ho il diabete.**	oh eel deeah-**bay**-tay
Low cholesterol?	**Basso colesterolo?**	**bah**-soh koh-lay-stay-**roh**-loh
No caffeine.	**Senza caffeina.**	**sehn**-sah kah-fay**ee**-nah
No alcohol.	**Niente alcool.**	nee**ehn**-tay **ahl**-kohl
I am a...	**Sono un...**	**soh**-noh oon
...vegetarian.	**...vegetariano[a].**	vay-jay-tah-ree**ah**-noh
...strict vegetarian.	**...strettamente vegetariano[a].**	stray-tah-**mayn**-tay vay-jay-tah-ree**ah**-noh
...carnivore.	**...carnivoro[a].**	kar-**nee**-voh-roh

Tableware and condiments:

plate	**piatto**	pee**ah**-toh
napkin	**tovagliolo**	toh-vahl-**yoh**-loh
knife	**coltello**	kohl-**tehl**-loh
fork	**forchetta**	for-**kay**-tah
spoon	**cucchiaio**	koo-kee**ah**-yoh
cup	**tazza**	**taht**-sah
glass	**bicchiere**	bee-kee**ay**-ray

carafe	**caraffa**	kah-**rah**-fah
water	**acqua**	**ah**-kwah
bread	**pane**	**pah**-nay
breadsticks	**grissini**	gree-**see**-nee
butter	**burro**	**boo**-roh
margarine	**margarina**	mar-gah-**ree**-nah
salt / pepper	**sale / pepe**	**sah**-lay / **pay**-pay
sugar	**zucchero**	**tsoo**-kay-roh
artificial sweetener	**dolcificante**	dohl-chee-fee-**kahn**-tay
honey	**miele**	mee**ay**-lay
mustard	**senape**	**say**-nah-pay
mayonnaise	**maionese**	mah-yoh-**nay**-zay

EATING

Restaurant requests and regrets:

A little.	**Un po.'**	oon poh
More.	**Un altro po.'**	oon **ahl**-troh poh
Another.	**Un altro.**	oon **ahl**-troh
The same.	**Uguale.**	oo-**gwah**-lay
I did not order this.	**Io questo non l'ho ordinato.**	**eeoh kway**-stoh nohn loh or-dee-**nah**-toh
Is it included with the meal?	**È incluso nel pasto questo?**	eh een-**kloo**-zoh nayl **pah**-stoh **kway**-stoh
I'm in a hurry.	**Sono di fretta.**	**soh**-noh dee **fray**-tah
I must leave by...	**Devo anare via alle...**	**day**-voh ah-**nah**-ray **vee**-ah **ah**-lay
When will the food be ready?	**Tra quanto è pronto il cibo?**	trah **kwahn**-toh eh **pron**-toh eel **chee**-boh
I've changed my mind.	**Ho cambiato idea.**	oh kahm-bee**ah**-toh ee-**day**-ah

Can I get it "to go"?	**Posso averlo da portar via?**	**pos**-soh ah-**vehr**-loh dah **por**-tar **vee**-ah
This is...	**Questo è...**	**kway**-stoh eh
...dirty.	**...sporco.**	**spor**-koh
...greasy.	**...grasso.**	**grah**-soh
...too salty.	**...troppo salato.**	**trop**-poh sah-**lah**-toh
...undercooked.	**...troppo crudo.**	**trop**-poh **kroo**-doh
...overcooked.	**...troppo cotto.**	**trop**-poh **kot**-toh
...inedible.	**...immangiabile.**	eem-mahn-**jah**-bee-lay
...cold.	**...freddo.**	**fray**-doh
Heat it up?	**Lo può scaldare?**	loh pwoh skahl-**dah**-ray
Enjoy your meal!	**Buon appetito!**	bwohn ah-pay-**tee**-toh
Enough.	**Basta.**	**bah**-stah
Finished.	**Finito.**	fee-**nee**-toh
Do any of your customers return?	**Ritornano i vostri clienti?**	ree-**tor**-nah-noh ee **voh**-stree klee-**ehn**-tee
Yuck!	**Che schifo!**	kay **skee**-foh
Delicious!	**Delizioso!**	day-leet-see**oh**-zoh
Divinely good!	**Una vera bontà!**	**oo**-nah **vay**-rah bohn-**tah**
My compliments to the chef!	**Complimenti al cuoco!**	kohm-plee-**mayn**-tee ahl koo**oh**-koh

Paying for your meal:

Waiter.	**Cameriere.**	kah-may-reeay-ray
Waitress.	**Cameriera.**	kah-may-reeay-rah
The bill, please.	**Il conto, per favore.**	eel **kohn**-toh pehr fah-**voh**-ray
Together.	**Conto unico.**	**kohn**-toh **oo**-nee-koh
Separate checks.	**Conto separato.**	**kohn**-toh say-pah-**rah**-toh
Credit card O.K.?	**Carta di credito è O.K.?**	**kar**-tah dee **kray**-dee-toh eh "O.K."
Is there a cover charge?	**Si paga per il coperto?**	see **pah**-gah pehr eel koh-**pehr**-toh
Is service included?	**È incluso il servizio?**	eh een-**kloo**-zoh eel sehr-**veet**-seeoh
This is not correct.	**Questo non è giusto.**	**kway**-stoh nohn eh **joo**-stoh
Explain it?	**Lo può spiegare?**	loh pwoh speeay-**gah**-ray
What if I wash the dishes?	**E se lavassi i piatti?**	ay say lah-**vah**-see ee pee**ah**-tee
Keep the change.	**Tenga il resto.**	**tayn**-gah eel **rehs**-toh
This is for you.	**Questo è per lei.**	**kway**-stoh eh pehr **leh**ee

EATING

In Italian bars and freeway rest stops, pay first at the *cassa* (cash register), then take your receipt to the counter to get your food. In restaurants, you'll get the bill only when you ask for it. The menu will state if the *servizio* (tip) is included. Tipping beyond this is not expected, but it's polite to leave some coins. If the service has been super, toss in an extra 1000 *lire* per person at your table.

Breakfast:

breakfast	**colazione**	koh-laht-see**oh**-nay
bread	**pane**	**pah**-nay
roll	**brioche**	bree-**osh**
toast	**toast**	tost
butter	**burro**	**boo**-roh
jam	**marmellata**	mar-mehl-**lah**-tah
jelly	**gelatina**	jay-lah-**tee**-nah
pastry	**pasticcini**	pah-stee-**chee**-nee
croissant	**cornetto**	kor-**nay**-toh
omelet	**omelette, frittata**	oh-may-**leht**-tay, free-**tah**-tah
eggs...	**uova...**	**woh**-vah
...fried / scrambled	**...fritte / strapazzate**	**free**-tay / strah-paht-**sah**-tay
boiled egg...	**uovo alla coque...**	**woh**-voh **ah**-lah kok
...soft / hard	**...molle / sodo**	**mol**-lay / **soh**-doh
ham	**prosciutto cotto**	proh-**shoo**-toh **kot**-toh
cheese	**formaggio**	for-**mah**-joh
yogurt	**yogurt**	**yoh**-goort
cereal (any kind)	**corn flex**	korn flehx
milk	**latte**	**lah**-tay
hot chocolate	**cioccolata calda**	choh-koh-**lah**-tah **kahl**-dah
fruit juice	**succo di frutta**	**soo**-koh dee **froo**-tah
fresh orange juice	**spremuta di arancia**	spray-**moo**-tah dee ah-**rahn**-chah

coffee / tea (see Drinking)	**caffè / tè**	kah-**feh** / teh
Is breakfast included (in the room cost)?	**La colazione è inclusa?**	lah koh-laht-seeoh-nay eh een-**kloo**-zah

Italian breakfasts, like Italian bath towels, are small: coffee and a roll with butter and marmalade. The strong coffee is often mixed about half and half with milk. At your hotel, refills are usually free. The delicious red orange juice is made from Sicilian blood oranges (*arancia tarocco*). Local open-air markets thrive in the morning, and a picnic breakfast followed by a *cappuccino* in a bar is a good option.

Appetizers and snacks:

antipasto misto	mixed appetizers (usually meat)
bruschetta	toast with tomatoes and garlic
crostini Fiorentina	toast with liver paté
crostini Napoletana	toast with cheese
formaggi misti	assorted cheeses
panini	sandwiches
prosciutto e melone	cured ham with melon
salame	cured pork sausage
toast al prosciutto e formaggio	toast with ham and cheese
tramezzini vari	assorted small sandwiches

Pizza and quick meals:

For fresh, fast, and frugal pizza, **Pizza Rustica** shops offer the cheapest hot meal in any Italian town, selling pizza by the slice (*pezzo*) or weight (*etto* = 100 grams, around a quarter pound). **Due etti** (200 grams) make a good light lunch. You can eat your pizza on the spot, or order it *"Da portar via"* (for the road). For handier pizza, nearly any bar has lousy, microwavable pizza snacks. To get cold pizza warmed up, say, *"Calda"* (hot) or *"Molto calda"* (very hot) and throw in *"per favore"* (please). To get an extra plate, ask for a *"piatto extra."* Pizza words include:

acciughe	anchovies
calzone	folded pizza with various fillings
capricciosa	chef's specialty
carciofini	artichokes
funghi	mushrooms
Margherita	cheese and tomato sauce
Napoletana	cheese, anchovies and tomato sauce
peperoni	green or red peppers (not sausage!)
prosciutto	cured ham
Quattro Stagioni	4 toppings on separate quarters of a pizza
salamino piccante	pepperoni

For other quick, tasty meals, drop by a **Rosticceria**—a deli where you'll find a cafeteria-style display of reasonably priced food. Get it "to go" or take a seat and eat.

Soups and salads:

soup	**minestra, zuppa**	mee-**nehs**-trah, **tsoo**-pah
soup of the day	**zuppa del giorno**	**tsoo**-pah dayl **jor**-noh
broth...	**brodo...**	**brod**-oh
...chicken	**...di pollo**	dee **poh**-loh
...beef	**...di carne**	dee **kar**-nay
...vegetable	**...di verdura**	dee vehr-**doo**-rah
...with noodles	**...con pastina**	kohn pah-**stee**-nah
...with rice	**...con riso**	kohn **ree**-zoh
vegetable soup	**minestrone**	mee-nay-**stroh**-nay
green salad	**insalata verde**	een-sah-**lah**-tah **vehr**-day
mixed salad	**insalata mista**	een-sah-**lah**-tah **mee**-stah
seafood salad	**insalata di mare**	een-sah-**lah**-tah dee **mah**-ray
chef's salad...	**insalata dello chef...**	een-sah-**lah**-tah **day**-loh shehf
...with ham and cheese	**...con prosciutto e formaggio**	kohn proh-**shoo**-toh ay for-**mah**-joh
...with egg	**...con uova**	kohn **woh**-vah
lettuce	**lattuga**	lah-**too**-gah
tomatoes	**pomodori**	poh-moh-**doh**-ree
cucumber	**cetrioli**	chay-tree**oh**-lee
oil / vinegar	**olio / aceto**	**oh**-leeoh / ah-**chay**-toh
What is in this salad?	**Che cosa c'è in questa insalata?**	kay **koh**-zah cheh een **kway**-stah een-sah-**lah**-tah

In Italian restaurants, salad dressing is normally just the oil and vinegar at the table. Salad bars at fast food restaurants and *autostrada* rest stops can be a good budget bet.

Pasta:

Italy is the land of *pasta*. You can taste over 500 types! While there are a few differences in ingredients, the big deal is basically the shape. Watch for *rigatone* (little tubes), *canneloni* (big tubes), *fettucine* (flat noodles), *farfalline* (butterfly-shaped pasta), *gnocchi* (shell-shaped noodles made from potatoes), *linguine* (thin, flat noodles), *penne* (angle-cut tubes), *rotelline* (wheel-shaped pasta), *tagliatelle* (short, flat noodles), *toscanini* (slender conductor), and *tortellini* (pasta "doughnuts" filled with meat or cheese), and surprise...*spaghetti*. Pasta can be stuffed *ravioli*-style with various meats, cheeses, herbs, and spices. Pasta sauces and styles include:

amatriciana	Roman-style with bacon, tomato, and spices
bolognese	meat and tomato sauce
carbonara	bacon, egg, cream, and pepper
genovese	pesto
in brodo	in broth
marinara	tomato and garlic
panna	cream
pescatora	seafood
pesto	olive oil, garlic, pine nuts, and basil
pomodoro	tomato only
quattro formaggi	four cheeses
ragù	meaty tomato sauce
sugo	sauce, usually tomato
vongole	with clams and spices

Italian specialities:

cozze ripiene	mussels stuffed with bread, cheese, garlic, and tomatoes
focaccia	flat bread with herbs
insalata caprese	salad of mozzarella, tomatoes, and basil
pancetta	thick bacon
polenta	moist cornmeal (Venice)
ribollita	cabbage and bean soup (Tuscany)
risotto	saffron rice dish with meat, seafood, or vegetables (Northern Italy)
saltimbocca	veal wrapped in ham (Rome)
tramezzini	crustless filled sandwiches

EATING

Seafood:

seafood	**frutti di mare**	**froo**-tee dee **mah**-ray
assorted seafood	**misto di frutti di mare**	**mee**-stoh dee **froo**-tee dee **mah**-ray
fish	**pesce**	**pay**-shay
cod	**merluzzo**	mehr-**loot**-soh
salmon	**salmone**	sahl-**moh**-nay
sole	**sogliola**	sohl-**yoh**-lah
trout	**trota**	**trot**-ah
tuna	**tonno**	**toh**-noh
herring	**aringa**	ah-**reeng**-gah
sardines	**sarde**	**sar**-day

anchovies	**acciughe**	ah-**choo**-gay
clams	**vongole**	**vohn**-goh-lay
mussels	**cozze**	**kot**-say
oysters	**ostriche**	**os**-tree-kay
shrimp	**gamberetti**	gahm-bay-**ray**-tee
prawns	**scampi**	**skahm**-pee
crab	**granchione**	grahn-kee**oh**-nay
lobster	**aragosta**	ah-rah-**goh**-stah
squid	**calamari**	kah-lah-**mah**-ree
Where did this live?	**Da dove viene questo?**	dah **doh**-vay veeay-nay **kway**-stoh
Just the head, please.	**Solo la testa, per favore.**	**soh**-loh lah **tehs**-tah pehr fah-**voh**-ray

Poultry and meat:

poultry	**pollame**	poh-**lah**-may
chicken	**pollo**	**poh**-loh
turkey	**tacchino**	tah-**kee**-noh
duck	**anatra**	**ah**-nah-trah
meat	**carne**	**kar**-nay
beef	**manzo**	**mahnd**-zoh
roast beef	**roast beef**	"roast beef"
beef steak	**bistecca di manzo**	bee-**stay**-kah dee **mahnd**-zoh
T-bone steak	**bistecca Fiorentina**	bee-**stay**-kah fee-oh-rehn-**tee**-nah

sirloin steak	**entrecote**	ayn-tray-**koh**-tay
meat stew	**stufato di carne**	stoo-**fah**-toh dee **kar**-nay
veal	**vitello**	vee-**tehl**-loh
thin-sliced veal	**scaloppine**	skah-loh-**pee**-nay
cutlet (veal)	**cotoletta**	koh-toh-**lay**-tah
pork	**maiale**	mah-**yah**-lay
cured ham	**prosciutto**	proh-**shoo**-toh
sausage	**salsiccia**	sahl-**see**-chah
lamb	**agnello**	ahn-**yehl**-loh
bunny	**coniglio**	koh-**neel**-yoh
brains	**cervello**	chehr-**vehl**-loh
sweetbreads	**animelle di vitello**	ah-nee-**mehl**-lay dee vee-**tehl**-loh
tongue	**lingua**	**leeng**-gwah
liver	**fegato**	**fay**-gah-toh
tripe	**trippa**	**tree**-pah
How long has this been dead?	**Da quanto tempo è morto questo?**	dah **kwahn**-toh **tehm**-poh eh **mor**-toh **kway**-stoh

EATING

Avoiding mis-steaks:

raw	**crudo**	**kroo**-doh
rare	**al sangue**	ahl **sahn**-gway
medium	**cotto**	**kot**-toh
well done	**ben cotto**	bayn **kot**-toh
almost burnt	**quasi bruciato**	**kwah**-zee broo-**chah**-toh

On a menu, the price of steak is often listed per *etto* (100 grams).

How it's prepared:

hot / cold	**caldo / freddo**	**kahl**-doh / **fray**-doh
raw / cooked	**crudo / cotto**	**kroo**-doh / **kot**-toh
assorted	**assortiti**	ah-sor-**tee**-tee
baked	**al forno**	ahl **for**-noh
boiled	**bollito**	boh-**lee**-toh
fillet	**filetto**	fee-**lay**-toh
fresh	**fresco**	**fray**-skoh
fried	**fritto**	**free**-toh
fried with breadcrumbs	**Milanese**	mee-lah-**nay**-zay
grilled	**alla griglia**	**ah**-lah **greel**-yah
homemade	**casalingo**	kah-zah-**leen**-goh
in cream sauce	**con panna**	kohn **pah**-nah
microwave	**forno a micro onde**	**for**-noh ah **mee**-kroh **ohn**-day
mild	**saporito**	sah-poh-**ree**-toh
mixed	**misto**	**mee**-stoh
poached	**affogato**	ah-foh-**gah**-toh
roasted	**arrosto**	ah-**roh**-stoh
sautéed	**saltato in padella**	sahl-**tah**-toh een pah-**dehl**-lah
smoked	**affumicato**	ah-foo-mee-**kah**-toh
spicy hot	**piccante**	pee-**kahn**-tay
steamed	**al vapore**	ahl vah-**poh**-ray
stuffed	**ripieno**	ree-peeay-noh
sweet	**dolce**	**dohl**-chay
with cheese and breadcrumbs	**alla Parmigiana**	**ah**-lah par-mee-**jah**-nah

Veggies, beans, and rice:

vegetables	legumi, verdure	lay-**goo**-mee, vehr-**doo**-ray
mixed vegetables	misto di verdure	**mee**-stoh dee vehr-**doo**-ray
artichoke	carciofo	kar-**choh**-foh
asparagus	asparagi	ah-spah-**rah**-jee
beans	fagioli	fah-**joh**-lee
beets	barbabietole	bar-bah-beeay-**toh**-lay
broccoli	broccoli	**brok**-koh-lee
cabbage	verza	**vehrt**-sah
carrots	carote	kah-**rot**-ay
cauliflower	cavolfiore	kah-vohl-feeoh-ray
corn	granturco	grahn-**toor**-koh
cucumber	cetrioli	chay-treeoh-lee
eggplant	melanzana	may-lahnt-**sah**-nah
French fries	patate fritte	pah-**tah**-tay **free**-tay
garlic	aglio	**ahl**-yoh
green beans	fagiolini	fah-joh-**lee**-nee
lentils	lenticchie	lehn-**tee**-keeay
mushrooms	funghi	**foong**-gee
olives	olive	oh-**lee**-vay
onions	cipolle	chee-**poh**-lay
peas	piselli	pee-**zehl**-lee
peppers...	peperoni...	pay-pay-**roh**-nee
...green / red	...verdi / rossi	**vehr**-dee / **roh**-see
pickles	cetriolini	chay-treeoh-**lee**-nee
potatoes	patate	pah-**tah**-tay
rice	riso	**ree**-zoh
spinach	spinaci	spee-**nah**-chee
tomatoes	pomodori	poh-moh-**doh**-ree
zucchini	zucchine	tsoo-**kee**-nay

EATING

Say cheese:

cheese	**formaggio**	for-**mah**-joh
mild and soft	**fresco**	**fray**-skoh
sharp and hard	**stagionato**	stah-joh-**nah**-toh
mozzarella	**mozzarella**	moht-sah-**ray**-lah
small mozzarella balls	**latticini**	lah-tee-**chee**-nee
goat	**di capra**	dee **kah**-prah
sheep cheese	**pecorino**	pay-koh-**ree**-noh
bleu cheese	**gorgonzola**	gor-gohnd-**zoh**-lah
cream cheese	**formaggio philadelphia**	for-**mah**-joh fee-lah-**dehl**-feeah
Swiss cheese	**groviera, emmenthal**	groh-veeay-rah, ehm-mehn-**tahl**
parmesan	**parmigiano**	par-mee-**jah**-noh
a soft white cheese	**Bel Paese**	behl pah-**ay**-zay
a tasty spreadable cheese	**stracchino**	strah-**kee**-noh
A little taste?	**Un assaggio?**	oon ah-**sah**-joh

Fruits and nuts:

almond	**mandorle**	mahn-**dor**-lay
apple	**mela**	**may**-lah
apricot	**albicocca**	ahl-bee-**koh**-kah
banana	**banana**	bah-**nah**-nah
berries	**frutti di bosco**	**froo**-tee dee **bos**-koh
canteloupe	**melone**	may-**loh**-nay
cherry	**ciliegia**	chee-leeay-jah

chestnut	**castagne**	kah-**stahn**-yay
coconut	**noce di cocco**	**noh**-chay dee **koh**-koh
dates	**datteri**	**dah**-tay-ree
fig	**fico**	**fee**-koh
fruit	**frutta**	**froo**-tah
grapefruit	**pompelmo**	pohm-**payl**-moh
grapes	**uva**	**oo**-vah
hazelnut	**nocciola**	noh-**choh**-lah
lemon	**limone**	lee-**moh**-nay
orange	**arancia**	ah-**rahn**-chah
peach	**pesca**	**pehs**-kah
peanut	**noccioline**	noh-choh-**lee**-nay
pear	**pera**	**pay**-rah
pineapple	**ananas**	**ah**-nah-nahs
pistachio	**pistacchio**	pee-**stah**-keeoh
plum	**susina**	soo-**zee**-nah
prune	**prugna**	**proon**-yah
raspberry	**lampone**	lahm-**poh**-nay
strawberry	**fragola**	**frah**-goh-lah
tangerine	**mandarino**	mahn-dah-**ree**-noh
walnut	**noce**	**noh**-chay
watermelon	**cocomero**	koh-koh-**may**-roh

EATING

On a menu, you might see *"frutta fresca di stagione"* (fresh fruit of the season).

Just desserts:

dessert	**dolci**	**dohl**-chee
cake	**torta**	**tor**-tah
ice cream	**gelato**	jay-**lah**-toh
sherbet	**sorbetto**	sor-**bay**-toh

fruit cup	**coppa di frutta**	**kop**-pah dee **froo**-tah
tart	**tartina**	tar-**tee**-nah
pie	**torte**	**tor**-tay
whipped cream	**panna**	**pah**-nah
chocolate mousse	**mousse**	moos
pudding	**budino**	boo-**dee**-noh
pastry	**pasticcini**	pah-stee-**chee**-nee
strudel	**strudel**	**stroo**-dehl
cookies	**biscotti**	bee-**skot**-tee
candy	**caramelle**	kah-rah-**mehl**-lay
low calorie	**poche calorie**	**poh**-kay kah-loh-**ree**-ay
homemade	**casalingo**	kah-zah-**leen**-goh
Exquisite.	**Squisito.**	skwee-**zee**-toh
Sinfully good.	**Un peccato**	oon pay-**kah**-toh
(a sin of the throat)	**di gola.**	dee **goh**-lah
So good I even licked	**Così buono che**	koh-**zee** bwoh-noh kay
my moustache.	**mi sono leccato[a]**	mee **soh**-noh lay-**kah**-toh
	anche i baffi.	**ahn**-kay ee **bah**-fee

More Italian treats:

bignole con crema	cream puffs (Florence)
cassata	ice cream, sponge cake, ricotta cheese, fruit, & pistachios (Sicily)
granita	snow-cone
panforte	dense fruit & nut cake (Siena)
tartufo	super-chocolate ice cream (Rome)
tiramisú	espresso-soaked cake with chocolate, cream, & brandy
zabaglione	delicious egg & liquor cream
zuppa inglese	rum-soaked cake with whipped cream

Gelati talk:

cone / cup	**cono / coppa**	**koh**-noh / **kop**-pah
one scoop	**una pallina**	**oo**-nah pah-**lee**-nah
two scoops	**due palline**	**doo**-ay pah-**lee**-nay
with whipped cream	**con panna**	kohn **pah**-nah
A little taste?	**Un assaggio?**	oon ah-**sah**-joh
How many flavors can I get per scoop?	**Quanti gusti posso avere per pallina?**	**kwahn**-tee **goo**-stee **pos**-soh ah-**vay**-ray pehr pah-**lee**-nah
apricot	**albicocca**	ahl-bee-**koh**-kah
berries	**frutti di bosco**	**froo**-tee dee **bos**-koh
blueberry	**mirtillo**	meer-**tee**-loh
cantaloupe	**melone**	may-**loh**-nay
chocolate	**cioccolato**	choh-koh-**lah**-toh
vanilla and chocolate chips	**stracciatella**	strah-chah-**tehl**-lah
chocolate hazelnut	**bacio**	**bah**-choh
coffee	**caffè**	kah-**feh**
hazelnut	**nocciola**	noh-**choh**-lah
lemon	**limone**	lee-**moh**-nay
mint	**menta**	**mayn**-tah
orange	**arancia**	ah-**rahn**-chah
peach	**pesca**	**pehs**-kah
pear	**pera**	**pay**-rah
pineapple	**ananas**	**ah**-nah-nahs
raspberry	**lampone**	lahm-**poh**-nay

rice	**riso**	**ree**-zoh
strawberry	**fragola**	**frah**-goh-lah
super chocolate	**tartufo**	tar-**too**-foh
vanilla	**crema**	**kray**-mah

Bacio (chocolate hazelnut) also means "kiss." *Baci* (kisses) are Italy's version of Chinese fortune cookies. The poetic fortunes, wrapped around chocolate balls, are written by people whose love of romance exceeds their grasp of English.

Drinking

Water, milk, and juice:

mineral water...	**acqua minerale...**	ah-kwah mee-nay-**rah**-lay
...carbonated	**...gassata**	gah-**sah**-tah
...not carbonated	**...non gassata**	nohn gah-**sah**-tah
tap water	**acqua del rubinetto**	ah-kwah dayl roo-bee-**nay**-toh
milk...	**latte...**	**lah**-tay
...whole	**...intero**	een-**tay**-roh
...skim	**...magro**	**mah**-groh
...fresh	**...fresco**	**fray**-skoh
milk shake	**frappè**	frah-**peh**
hot chocolate	**cioccolata calda**	choh-koh-**lah**-tah **kahl**-dah
orange soda	**aranciata**	ah-rahn-**chah**-tah
lemon soda	**limonata**	lee-moh-**nah**-tah
juice...	**succo...**	**soo**-koh
...fruit	**...di frutta**	dee **froo**-tah
...apple	**...di mela**	dee **may**-lah
...orange	**...di arancia**	dee ah-**rahn**-chah
freshly-squeezed orange juice	**spremuta d'arancia**	spray-**moo**-tah dah-**rahn**-chah
with / without...	**con / senza...**	kohn / **sehn**-sah
...ice / sugar	**...ghiaccio / zucchero**	geeah-choh / **tsoo**-kay-roh
glass / cup	**bicchiere / tazza**	bee-keeay-ray / **taht**-sah

EATING

bottle...	**bottiglia...**	boh-**teel**-yah
...small / large	**...piccola / grande**	**pee**-koh-lah / **grahn**-day
Is this water safe to drink?	**È potabile quest'acqua?**	eh poh-**tah**-bee-lay kway-**stah**-kwah

I drink the tap water in Italy (Venice's is piped in from a mountain spring, and Florence's is very chlorinated), but it's good style and never expensive to order a *litro* (liter) or *mezzo litro* (half liter) of bottled water with your meal.

Coffee and tea:

coffee...	**caffè...**	kah-**feh**
...with water	**...lungo**	**loon**-goh
...with a little milk	**...macchiato**	mah-keeah-toh
...with milk	**...latte**	**lah**-tay
...iced	**...freddo**	**fray**-doh
...instant	**...solubile**	soo-**loo**-bee-lay
...American-style	**...Americano**	ah-may-ree-**kah**-noh
coffee with foamy milk	**cappuccino**	kah-poo-**chee**-noh
decaffeinated	**decaffeinato, Hag**	day-kah-fay-**nah**-toh, hahg
black	**nero**	**nay**-roh
milk...	**latte...**	**lah**-tay
...with a little coffee	**...macchiato**	mah-keeah-toh
sugar	**zucchero**	**tsoo**-kay-roh
hot water	**acqua calda**	**ah**-kwah **kahl**-dah
tea / lemon	**tè / limone**	teh / lee-**moh**-nay

tea bag	**bustina di tè**	boo-**stee**-nah dee teh
herbal tea (decaf)	**tè decaffeinato**	teh day-kah-fay-**nah**-toh
iced tea	**tè freddo**	teh **fray**-doh
small / large	**piccola / grande**	**pee**-koh-lah / **grahn**-day
Another cup.	**Un'altra tazza.**	oo-**nahl**-trah **taht**-sah
Same price if I sit or stand?	**Costa uguale al tavolo o al banco?**	**kos**-tah oo-**gwah**-lay ahl **tah**-voh-loh oh ahl **bahn**-koh

EATING

Caffè is espresso served in a teeny tiny cup. Foamy *cappuccino* was named after the monks with their brown robes and frothy cowls. A *coretto* is coffee and firewater. In a bar, you'll pay at the *cassa*, then take your receipt to the person who makes the coffee. Refills are never free, except at hotel breakfasts.

When you're ordering coffee in bars in bigger cities, you'll notice that the price board clearly lists two price levels: the cheaper level for the stand-up *bar* and the more expensive for the *tavolo* (table) or *terrazza* (out on the terrace or sidewalk).

Wine:

I would like...	Vorrei....	vor-**rehee**
We would like...	Vorremo...	vor-**ray**-moh
...a glass	**...un bicchiere**	oon bee-kee**ay**-ray
...a quarter of a liter	**...un quarto litro**	oon **kwar**-toh **lee**-troh
...a half liter	**...un mezzo litro**	oon **mehd**-zoh **lee**-troh
...a carafe	**...una caraffa**	**oo**-nah kah-**rah**-fah
...a half bottle	**...una mezza bottiglia**	**oo**-nah **mehd**-zah boh-**teel**-yah
...a bottle	**...una bottiglia**	**oo**-nah boh-**teel**-yah
...of red wine	**...di rosso**	dee **roh**-soh
...of white wine	**...di bianco**	dee bee**ahn**-koh
...the wine list	**...la lista dei vini**	lah **lee**-stah **deh**ee **vee**-nee

Wine words:

wine / wines	**vino / vini**	**vee**-noh / **vee**-nee
house wine	**vino della casa**	**vee**-noh **day**-lah **kah**-zah
local	**locale**	loh-**kah**-lay
red	**rosso**	**roh**-soh
white	**bianco**	bee**ahn**-koh
rosé	**rosato**	roh-**zah**-toh
sparkling	**frizzante**	freet-**sahn**-tay
sweet	**dolce, abbocato**	**dohl**-chay, ah-boh-**kah**-toh
medium	**medio**	**may**-deeoh
dry	**secco**	**say**-koh
very dry	**molto secco**	**mohl**-toh **say**-koh
cork	**tappo**	**tah**-poh

Italy leads the world in wine production and you'll find it on nearly every table. To save money, order *"Una caraffa di vino della casa"* (a carafe of the house wine). Red wine dominates, as it should. Tuscany is famous for its *chianti*, but also has a good white wine, *Vernaccia*. *Orvieto Classico* is a popular white wine from Umbria. If you like a sweet after-dinner wine, don't miss the *Sciachetrà* from the *Cinque Terre.* Many small-town Italians in the hotel business have a cellar or cantina which they are proud to show off. They'll often jump at any excuse to descend and drink.

EATING

Beer:

beer	**birra**	**bee**-rah
from the tap	**alla spina**	ah-lah **spee**-nah
bottle	**bottiglia**	boh-**teel**-yah
light / dark	**chiara / scura**	keeah-rah / **skoo**-rah
local / imported	**locale / importata**	loh-**kah**-lay / eem-por-**tah**-tah
small / large	**piccola / grande**	**pee**-koh-lah / **grahn**-day
alcohol-free	**analcolica**	ahn-ahl-**koh**-lee-kah
cold	**fredda**	**fray**-dah
colder	**più fredda**	pew **fray**-dah

Bar talk:

What would you like?	**Che cosa prende?**	kay **koh**-zah **prehn**-day
What is the local specialty?	**Qual'è la specialità locale?**	kwah-**leh** lah spay-chah-lee-**tah** loh-**kah**-lay
Straight.	**Liscio.**	**lee**-shoh
With / Without...	**Con / Senza...**	kohn / **sehn**-sah
...alcohol.	**...alcool.**	**ahl**-kohl
...ice.	**...ghiaccio.**	geeah-choh
One more.	**Un altro.**	oon **ahl**-troh
Cheers!	**Cin cin!**	cheen cheen
To your health!	**Salute!**	sah-**loo**-tay
Long life!	**Lunga vita!**	**loong**-gah **vee**-tah
Long live Italy!	**Viva l'Italia!**	**vee**-vah lee-**tahl**-yah
I'm feeling...	**Mi sento...**	mee **sehn**-toh
...a little drunk.	**...un po' ubriaco[a].**	oon poh oo-breeah-koh
...blitzed. (colloq.)	**...ubriaco[a] fradicio[a].**	oo-breeah-koh frah-dee-choh

An Italian speciality is *Cinzano,* a red, white, or rosé vermouth. After dinner, try a *digestivo,* a liqueur thought to aid in digestion. For a flammable drink, get *grappa,* firewater distilled from grape skins and stems.

For a memorable and affordable adventure in Venice, have a "pub crawl" dinner. While *cicchetti* (bar munchies) aren't as common as they used to be, many bars (called *ciccheteria*) are still popular for their wide selection of often ugly, always tasty hors d'oeuvres on toothpicks.

Picnicking

At the market:

Is it self service?	**È self-service?**	eh "self-service"
Ripe for today?	**Per mangiare oggi?**	pehr mahn-**jah**-ray **oh**-jee
Does it need to be cooked?	**Bisogna cucinarlo prima di mangiarlo?**	bee-**zohn**-yah koo-chee-**nar**-loh **pree**-mah dee mahn-**jar**-loh
A little taste?	**Un assaggio?**	oon ah-**sah**-joh
Fifty grams.	**Cinquanta grammi.**	cheeng-**kwahn**-tah **grah**-mee
One hundred grams.	**Un etto.**	oon **eht**-toh
More. / Less.	**Più. / Meno.**	pew / **may**-noh
A piece.	**Un pezzo.**	oon **peht**-soh
A slice.	**Una fettina.**	**oo**-nah fay-**tee**-nah
Sliced.	**Tagliato a fettine.**	tahl-**yah**-toh ah fay-**tee**-nay
Can you make me a sandwich?	**Mi può fare un panino?**	mee pwoh **fah**-ray oon pah-**nee**-noh
To take out.	**Da portar via.**	dah **por**-tar **vee**-ah
Is there a park nearby?	**C'è un parco qui vicino?**	cheh oon **par**-koh kwee vee-**chee**-noh
May we picnic here?	**Va bene fare un picnic qui?**	vah **behn**-nay **fah**-ray oon **peek**-neek kwee
Enjoy your meal!	**Buon appetito!**	bwohn ah-pay-**tee**-toh

EATING

Picnic prose:

open air market	**mercato**	mehr-**kah**-toh
grocery store	**alimentari**	ah-lee-mayn-**tah**-ree
supermarket	**supermercato**	soo-pehr-mehr-**kah**-toh
picnic	**picnic**	**peek**-neek
sandwich or roll	**panino**	pah-**nee**-noh
bread	**pane**	**pah**-nay
cured ham	**prosciutto**	proh-**shoo**-toh
sausage	**salsiccia**	sahl-**see**-chah
cheese	**formaggio**	for-**mah**-joh
mustard...	**senape...**	**say**-nah-pay
mayonnaise...	**maionese...**	mah-yoh-**nay**-zay
...in a tube	**...in tubetto**	een too-**bay**-toh
yogurt	**yogurt**	**yoh**-goort
fruit	**frutta**	**froo**-tah
box of juice	**cartoccio di succo di frutta**	kar-**toh**-choh dee **soo**-koh dee **froo**-tah
spoon / fork...	**cucchiaio / forchetta...**	koo-keeah-yoh / for-**kay**-tah
...made of plastic	**...di plastica**	dee **plah**-stee-kah
cup / plate...	**bicchiere / piatto...**	bee-keeay-ray / peeah-toh
...made of paper	**...di carta**	dee **kar**-tah

Make your own sandwiches by getting the ingredients at a market. Order meat and cheese by the gram. One hundred grams (what the Italians call an *etto*) is about a quarter pound, enough for two sandwiches.

Italian-English Menu Decoder

This handy decoder won't list every word on the menu, but it'll get you *trota* (trout) instead of *trippa* (tripe).

abbocato sweet
acciughe anchovies
aceto vinegar
acqua minerale mineral water
affogato poached
affumicato smoked
aglio garlic
agnello lamb
al forno baked
albicocca apricot
alcool alcohol
amatriciana with bacon, tomato, & spices
ananas pineapple
anatra duck
antipasti appetizers
aragosta lobster
arancia orange
aranciata orange soda
aringa herring
arrosto roasted
asparagi asparagus
assortiti assorted
bacio chocolate hazelnut
barbabietole beets
bevande beverages
bianco white
bibite beverages

bicchiere glass
birra beer
biscotti cookies
bistecca beef steak
bistecca Fiorentina T-bone steak
bollito boiled
bolognese meat & tomato sauce
bottiglia bottle
brioche roll
brodo broth
bruschetta toast with tomatoes
budino pudding
burro butter
caffè coffee
calamari squid
caldo hot
calzone folded pizza
cannelloni large tube-shaped noodles
cappuccino coffee with foam
capra goat
caprese mozzarella & tomato salad
capricciosa chef's specialty
caraffa carafe
caramelle candy
carbonara with meat sauce
carciofo artichoke
carne meat

MENU DECODER

carote carrots
casa house
casalingo homemade
castagne chestnut
cavolfiore cauliflower
cena dinner
cervello brains
cetrioli cucumber
cetriolini pickles
cibo food
ciliegia cherry
cinese Chinese
cioccolata chocolate
cipolle onions
cocomero watermelon
colazione breakfast
con with
coniglio rabbit
cono cone
contorni side dishes
coperto cover charge
coppa small bowl
coretto coffee & firewater
cornetto croissant
cotoletta cutlet
cotto cooked
cozze mussels
crema vanilla
crudo raw
cucina cuisine
cuoco chef
da portar via "to go"
datteri dates

del giorno of the day
della casa of the house
di of
digestivo after-dinner drink
dolce sweet
dolci desserts
e and
emmenthal Swiss cheese
entrecote sirloin steak
etto one hundred grams
fagioli beans
fagiolini green beans
farfalline butterfly-shaped pasta
fatto in casa homemade
fegato liver
fettina slice
fettucine flat noodles
fico fig
filetto fillet
focaccia flat bread
formaggio cheese
fragola strawberry
frappè milkshake
freddo cold
fresco fresh
frittata omelet
fritto fried
frizzante sparkling
frutta fruit
frutti di mare seafood
frutti di bosco berries
funghi mushrooms
gamberetti shrimp

gassata carbonated
gelatina jelly
gelato Italian ice cream
genovese with pesto sauce
ghiaccio ice
giorno day
gnocchi potato noodles
gorgonzola bleu cheese
granchione crab
grande large
granita snow-cone
granturco corn
grappa firewater
griglia grilled
grissini breadsticks
groviera Swiss cheese
gusti flavors
importata imported
incluso included
insalata salad
lampone raspberry
latte milk
latticini small mozzarella balls
lattuga lettuce
leggero light
legumi vegetables
limonata lemon soda
limone lemon
lingua tongue
locale local
maiale pork
maionese mayonnaise
mandarino tangerine

mandorle almond
manzo beef
margarina margarine
marmellata jam
mela apple
melanzana eggplant
melone canteloupe
menta mint
menù turistico fixed-price menu
menù del giorno menu of the day
mercato open air market
merluzzo cod
mezzo half
miele honey
Milanese fried in breadcrumbs
minerale, acqua mineral water
minestra soup
minestrone vegetable soup
mirtillo blueberry
misto mixed
molto very
nero black
nocciola hazelnut
noccioline peanut
noce walnut
noce di cocco coconut
non not
non fumatori non-smoking
o or
olio oil
olive olives
omelette omelet
ostriche oysters

pallina scoop
pancetta thick bacon
pane bread
panforte fruitcake
panino roll, sandwich
panna cream, whipped cream
parmigiano parmesan cheese
pasticcini pastry
pastina noodles
patate potatoes
patate fritte French fries
penne tube-shaped noodles
pepe pepper
peperoni bell peppers
pera pear
percorino sheep cheese
pesca peach
pesce fish
pezzo piece
piatto plate
picante spicy hot
piccolo small
piselli peas
pistacchio pistachio
polenta moist cornmeal
pollame poultry
pollo chicken
pomodori tomatoes
pompelmo grapefruit
pranzo lunch
prima colazione breakfast
primo piatto first course
prosciutto cured ham

prugna prune
quattro four
ribollita hearty cabbage soup
rigatone tube-shaped noodles
ripieno stuffed
riso rice
risotto saffron-flavored rice
ristorante restaurant
rosato rosé
rosso red
rosticceria deli
rotelline wheel-shaped pasta
salame pork sausage
salamino piccante pepperoni
sale salt
salmone salmon
salsiccia sausage
saporito mild
sarde sardines
scaloppine thin-sliced veal
scampi prawns
secco dry
secondo piatto second course
senape mustard
senza without
servizio service charge
servizio incluso service included
servizio non incluso service not
  included
sogliola sole
sorbetto sherbet
specialità speciality
spinaci spinach

spremuta freshly-squeezed juice
spuntino snack
stagioni seasons (& pizza toppings)
stracchino spreadable cheese
stracciatella chocolate chips with vanilla
strapazzate scrambled
stufato stew
succo juice
sugo sauce, usually tomato
susina plum
tacchino turkey
tagliatelle flat noodles
tartina tart
tartufo super-chocolate ice cream
tavola calda fast food
tavolo table
tazza cup
tè tea
tonno tuna

torta cake
torte pie
tortellini stuffed noodles
tovagliolo napkin
tramezzini crustless sandwiches
trippa tripe
trota trout
uova eggs
uva grapes
vegetariano vegetarian
veloce fast
verde green
verdure vegetables
verza cabbage
vino wine
vitello veal
vongole clams
yogurt yoghurt
zucchero sugar
zuppa soup

Sightseeing

Where is...?	Dov'è...?	doh-**veh**
...the best view	...la vista più bella	lah **vee**-stah pew **behl**-lah
...the main square	...la piazza principale	lah pee**aht**-sah preen-chee-**pah**-lay
...the old town center	...il centro storico	eel **chehn**-troh **stoh**-ree-koh
...the museum	...il museo	eel moo-**zay**-oh
...the castle	...il castello	eel kah-**stehl**-loh
...the palace	...il palazzo	eel pah-**laht**-soh
...the ruins	...le rovine	lay roh-**vee**-nay
...a festival	...un festival	oon **fehs**-tee-vahl
...tourist information	...informazioni per turisti	een-for-maht-see**oh**-nee pehr too-**ree**-stee
Do you have...?	Avete...?	ah-**vay**-tay
...a map	...una cartina	**oo**-nah kar-**tee**-nah
...information	...informazioni	een-for-maht-see**oh**-nee
...a guidebook	...una guida	**oo**-nah **gwee**-dah
...a tour	...una gita	**oo**-nah **jee**-tah
...in English	...in inglese	een een-**glay**-zay
When is the next tour in English?	Quando è la prossima gita in inglese?	**kwahn**-doh eh lah **pros**-see-mah **jee**-tah een een-**glay**-zay
Is it free?	È gratis?	eh **grah**-tees
How much is it?	Quanto costa?	**kwahn**-toh **kos**-tah

Is there a discount for...?	**Fate sconti per...?**	**fah**-tay **skohn**-tee pehr
...youth	**...giovani**	joh-**vah**-nee
...students	**...studenti**	stoo-**dehn**-tee
...seniors	**...pensionati**	payn-seeoh-**nah**-tee
Is (the ticket) valid all day?	**È valido per tutto il giorno?**	eh **vah**-lee-doh pehr **too**-toh eel **jor**-noh
Can I get back in?	**Posso rientrare?**	**pos**-soh ree-ehn-**trah**-ray
What time does this open / close?	**A che ora apre / chiude?**	ah kay **oh**-rah **ah**-pray / keeoo-day
What time is the last entry?	**Quand'è l'ultima entrata?**	kwahn-**deh lool**-tee-mah ayn-**trah**-tah
PLEASE let me in.	**PER FAVORE, mi faccia entrare.**	pehr fah-**voh**-ray mee **fah**-chah ayn-**trah**-ray
I've traveled all the way from...	**Sono venuto[a] qui da...**	**soh**-noh vay-**noo**-toh kwee dah
I must leave tomorrow.	**Devo partire domani.**	**day**-voh par-**tee**-ray doh-**mah**-nee
I promise I'll be fast.	**Prometto che sarò veloce.**	proh-**may**-toh kay sah-**roh** vay-**loh**-chay

In the museum:

Where is...?	**Dov'è...?**	doh-**veh**
I'd like to see...	**Mi piacerebbe vedere...**	mee peeah-chay-**ray**-bay vay-**day**-ray
Photo / video O.K.?	**Foto / video è O.K.?**	**foh**-toh / **vee**-day-oh eh "O.K."

No flash / tripod.	**Vietato usare flash / trepiede.**	veeay-**tah**-toh oo-**zah**-ray flahsh / tray-peeay-day
I like it.	**Mi piace.**	mee peeah-chay
It's so...	**È così...**	eh koh-zee
...beautiful.	**...bello.**	**behl**-loh
...ugly.	**...brutto.**	**broo**-toh
...strange.	**...strano.**	**strah**-noh
...boring.	**...noioso.**	noh-**yoh**-zoh
...interesting.	**...interessante.**	een-tay-ray-**sahn**-tay
Wow!	**Che diamine!**	kay deeah-mee-nay
My feet hurt!	**Mi fanno male i piedi!**	mee **fah**-noh **mah**-lay ee peeay-dee
I'm exhausted!	**Sono stanco[a] morto[a]!**	**soh**-noh **stahn**-koh **mor**-toh

Many museums close in the afternoon from 13:00 until 15:00 or 16:00, and are closed all day on a weekday, usually Monday. Museums often stop selling tickets 45 minutes before closing. Historic churches usually open much earlier than museums.

Art and architecture:

art	**arte**	**ar**-tay
artist	**artista**	ar-**tee**-stah
painting	**quadro**	**kwah**-droh
self portrait	**autoritratto**	ow-toh-ree-**trah**-toh
sculptor	**scultore**	skool-**toh**-ray

sculpture	**scultura**	skool-**too**-rah
architect	**architetto**	ar-kee-**teht**-toh
architecture	**architettura**	ar-kee-teht-**too**-rah
original	**originale**	oh-ree-jee-**nah**-lay
restored	**restaurato**	ray-stow-**rah**-toh
B.C. / A.D.	**A.C. / D.C.**	ah chee / dee chee
century	**secolo**	**say**-koh-loh
style	**stile**	**stee**-lay
Abstract	**Astratto**	ah-**strah**-toh
Ancient	**Antico**	ahn-**tee**-koh
Art Nouveau	**Arte Nouveau**	**ar**-tay **noo**-voh
Baroque	**Barocco**	bah-**rok**-koh
Classical	**Classico**	**klah**-see-koh
Gothic	**Gotico**	**got**-ee-koh
Impressionist	**Impressionista**	eem-pray-seeoh-**nee**-stah
Medieval	**Medievale**	may-deeay-**vah**-lay
Modern	**Moderno**	moh-**dehr**-noh
Neoclassical	**Neoclassico**	nee-oh-**klah**-see-koh
Renaissance	**Rinascimento**	ree-nah-shee-**mayn**-toh
Romanesque	**Romanesco**	roh-mah-**nay**-skoh
Romantic	**Romantico**	roh-**mahn**-tee-koh

The Italians refer to their three greatest centuries of art in an unusual way. The 1300s are called *tre cento* (300s). The 1400s (early Renaissance) are called *quattro cento* (400s), and the 1500s (High Renaissance) are *cinque cento* (500s).

Castles and palaces:

castle	**castello**	kah-**stehl**-loh
palace	**palazzo**	pah-**laht**-soh
kitchen	**cucina**	koo-**chee**-nah
cellar	**cantina**	kahn-**tee**-nah
dungeon	**segrete**	say-**gray**-tay
moat	**fossato**	foh-**sah**-toh
fortified walls	**muri fortificati**	**moo**-ree for-tee-fee-**kah**-tee
tower	**torre**	**tor**-ray
fountain	**fontana**	fohn-**tah**-nah
garden	**giardino**	jar-**dee**-noh
king	**re**	ray
queen	**regina**	ray-**jee**-nah
knights	**cavalieri**	kah-vah-leeay-ree

Religious words:

cathedral	**duomo**	**dwoh**-moh
church	**chiesa**	keeay-zah
monastery	**monastero**	moh-nah-**stay**-roh
synagogue	**sinagoga**	see-nah-**gog**-ah
chapel	**cappella**	kah-**pehl**-lah
altar	**altare**	ahl-**tah**-ray
cross	**croce**	**kroh**-chay
treasury	**tesoro**	tay-**zoh**-roh

crypt	**cripta**	**kreep**-tah
dome	**cupola**	**koo**-poh-lah
bells	**campane**	kahm-**pah**-nay
organ	**organo**	**or**-gah-noh
relics	**reliquie**	ray-**lee**-kweeay
saint	**santo[a]**	**sahn**-toh
God	**Dio**	**dee**-oh
Jewish	**ebreo**	ay-**bray**-oh
Moslem	**mussulmano[a]**	moo-sool-**mah**-noh
Christian	**cristiano[a]**	kree-steeah-noh
Protestant	**protestante**	proh-tay-**stahn**-tay
Catholic	**cattolico[a]**	kah-**toh**-lee-koh
agnostic	**agnostico[a]**	ahn-**yoh**-stee-koh
atheist	**ateo[a]**	ah-**tay**-oh
When is the service?	**A che ora è la messa?**	ah kay **oh**-rah eh lah **may**-sah
Are there church concerts?	**Ci sono concerti in chiesa?**	chee **soh**-noh kohn-**chehr**-tee een keeay-zah

The piano was invented in Italy. Unlike a harpsichord, it could be played soft and loud, so it was called just that: *piano-forte* (soft-loud). Here are other Italian musical words you might remember: *subito* (suddenly), *crescendo* (growing louder), *sopra* (over), *sotto* (under), *ritardando* (slowing down), and *fine* (finish).

SIGHTSEEING

Shopping

Names of Italian shops:

antiques	**negozio di antiquariato**	nay-**goht**-seeoh dee ahn-tee-kwah-reeah-toh
art gallery	**galleria d'arte**	gah-lay-**ree**-ah **dar**-tay
bakery	**panificio**	pah-nee-**fee**-choh
barber shop	**barbiere**	bar-bee**ay**-ray
beauty salon	**parrucchiere**	pah-roo-kee**ay**-ray
book shop	**libreria**	lee-bray-**ree**-ah
camera shop	**foto-ottica**	foh-toh-**ot**-tee-kah
department store	**grande magazzino**	**grahn**-day mah-gahd-**zee**-noh
flea market	**mercato delle pulci**	mehr-**kah**-toh **day**-lay **pool**-chee
flower market	**mercato dei fiori**	mehr-**kah**-toh **deh**ee fee-**oh**-ree
grocery store	**alimentari**	ah-lee-mayn-**tah**-ree
hardware store	**ferramenta**	fehr-rah-**mehn**-tah
jewelry shop	**gioielliere**	joh-yay-lee**ay**-ray
laundromat	**lavanderia**	lah-vahn-day-**ree**-ah
newsstand	**giornalaio**	jor-nah-**lah**-yoh
office supplies	**cartoleria**	kar-toh-lay-**ree**-ah
open air market	**mercato**	mehr-**kah**-toh
optician	**ottico**	**ot**-tee-koh
pharmacy	**farmacia**	far-mah-**chee**-ah

photocopy shop	**copisteria**	koh-pee-stay-**ree**-ah
shopping mall	**centro commerciale**	**chehn**-troh koh-mehr-**chah**-lay
souvenir shop	**negozio di souvenir**	nay-**goht**-seeoh dee **soo**-vay-neer
supermarket	**supermercato**	soo-pehr-mehr-**kah**-toh
toy store	**negozio di giocattoli**	nay-**goht**-seeoh dee joh-**kah**-toh-lee
travel agency	**agenzia di viaggi**	ah-jehnt-**see**-ah dee vee**ah**-jee
used bookstore	**negozio di libri usati**	nay-**goht**-seeoh dee **lee**-bree oo-**zah**-tee
wine shop	**negozio di vini**	nay-**goht**-seeoh dee **vee**-nee

SHOPPING

Most businesses are closed daily from 13:00 until 15:00 or 16:00. Many stores in the larger cities close for all or part of August—not a good time to plan a shopping spree.

Shop till you drop:

sale	**saldo**	**sahl**-doh
How much is it?	**Quanto costa?**	**kwahn**-toh **kos**-tah
I'm / We're...	**Sto / Stiamo...**	stoh / stee**ah**-moh
...just browsing.	**...solo guardando.**	**soh**-loh gwar-**dahn**-doh
I'd like...	**Vorrei...**	vor-**rehee**
Do you have...?	**Avete...?**	ah-**vay**-tay
...something cheaper	**...qualcosa di meno caro**	kwahl-**koh**-zah dee **may**-noh **kah**-roh

Can I see more?	**Posso vederne ancora?**	pos-soh vay-**dehr**-nay ahn-**koh**-rah
This one.	**Questo qui.**	**kway**-stoh kwee
Can I try it on?	**Lo posso provare?**	loh **pos**-soh proh-**vah**-ray
Do you have a mirror?	**Ha uno specchio?**	ah **oo**-noh **spay**-keeoh
Too...	**Troppo...**	**trop**-poh
...big.	**...grande.**	**grahn**-day
...small.	**...piccolo.**	**pee**-koh-loh
...expensive.	**...caro.**	**kah**-roh
Did you make this?	**L'avete fatto voi questo?**	lah-**vay**-tay **fah**-toh vohee **kway**-stoh
What's it made out of?	**Di che cosa è fatto?**	dee kay **koh**-zah eh **fah**-toh
Is it machine washable?	**Si può lavare in lavatrice?**	see pwoh lah-**vah**-ray een lah-vah-**tree**-chay
Will it shrink?	**Si ritira?**	see ree-**tee**-rah
Credit card O.K.?	**Carta di credito è O.K.?**	**kar**-tah dee **kray**-dee-toh eh "O.K."
Can you ship this?	**Può spedirmelo?**	pwoh spay-deer-**may**-loh
Tax-free?	**Esente da tasse?**	ay-**zehn**-tay dah **tah**-say
I'll think about it.	**Ci penserò.**	chee pehn-say-**roh**
What time do you close?	**A che ora chiudete?**	ah kay **oh**-rah keeoo-**day**-tay
What time do you open tomorrow?	**A che ora aprite domani?**	ah kay **oh**-rah ah-**pree**-tay doh-**mah**-nee
Is that your final price?	**È questo il prezzo finale?**	eh **kway**-stoh eel **preht**-soh fee-**nah**-lay

My last offer.	**La mia ultima offerta.**	lah **mee**-ah **ool**-tee-mah oh-**fehr**-tah
I'm nearly broke.	**Sono quasi al verde.**	**soh**-noh **kwah**-zee ahl **vehr**-day
My male friend...	**Il mio amico...**	eel **mee**-oh ah-**mee**-koh
My female friend...	**La mia amica...**	lah **mee**-ah ah-**mee**-kah
My husband...	**Mio marito...**	**mee**-oh mah-**ree**-toh
My wife...	**Mia moglie...**	**mee**-ah **mohl**-yay
...has the money.	**...ha i soldi.**	ah ee **sohl**-dee

You can look up colors and fabrics in the dictionary near the end of this book.

Repair:

These handy lines can apply to any repair, whether it's a stuck zipper, a broken leg, or a dying car.

This is broken.	**Questo è rotto.**	**kway**-stoh eh **rot**-toh
Can you fix it?	**Lo può aggiustare?**	loh pwoh ah-joo-**stah**-ray
Just do the essentials.	**Faccia solamente le cose essenziali.**	**fah**-chah soh-lah-**mayn**-tay lay **koh**-zay ay-saynt-seeah-lee
How much will it cost?	**Quanto costa?**	**kwahn**-toh **kos**-tah
When will it be ready?	**Quando è pronta?**	**kwahn**-doh eh **pron**-tah
I need it by ___.	**Ne ho bisogno entro ___.**	nay oh bee-**zohn**-yoh **ayn**-troh

Entertainment

What's happening tonight?	**Che cosa succede stasera?**	kay **koh**-zah soo-**chay**-day stah-**zay**-rah
What do you recommend?	**Che cosa raccomanda?**	kay **koh**-zah rah-koh-**mahn**-dah
Is it free?	**È gratis?**	eh **grah**-tees
Where can I buy a ticket?	**Dove si comprano i biglietti?**	**doh**-vay see kohm-**prah**-noh ee beel-**yay**-tee
When does it start?	**A che ora comincia?**	ah kay **oh**-rah koh-**meen**-chah
When does it end?	**A che ora finisce?**	ah kay **oh**-rah fee-**nee**-shay
Will you go out with me?	**Vuole uscire con me?**	**vwoh**-lay oo-**shee**-ray kohn may
Where's the best place to dance nearby?	**Qual'è il posto migliore per ballare qui vicino?**	kwah-**leh** eel **poh**-stoh meel-**yoh**-ray pehr bah-**lah**-ray kwee vee-**chee**-noh
Do you want to dance?	**Vuoi ballare?**	**vwoh**ee bah-**lah**-ray
Let's have a wild and crazy night!	**Diamoci una notte da sballo!**	deeah-**moh**-chee **oo**-nah **not**-tay dah **zbah**-loh
Where do people stroll?	**Dov'è la passeggiata?**	doh-**veh** lah pah-say-**jah**-tah

For cheap entertainment, join the locals and take a *passeggiata* (stroll) through town. As you bump shoulders in the crowd, you'll know why it's also called *struscio* (rubbing). On workdays, Italians stroll between work and dinner. On holidays, they hit the streets after lunch. This is Italy on parade. People are strutting. If ever you could enjoy being forward, this is the time. Whispering a breathy **bella** (cute girl) or **bello** (cute guy) feels natural.

Entertaining words:

movie...	**cinema...**	**chee**-nay-mah
...original version	**...versione originale**	vehr-seeoh-nay oh-ree-jee-**nah**-lay
...in English	**...in inglese**	een een-**glay**-zay
...with subtitles	**...con sottotitoli**	kohn soh-toh-**tee**-toh-lee
...dubbed	**...doppiato**	doh-peeah-toh
music...	**musica...**	**moo**-zee-kah
...live	**...dal vivo**	dahl **vee**-voh
...classical	**...classica**	**klah**-see-kah
...folk	**...folk**	fohlk
old rock	**rock vecchio stile**	rok **vehk**-eeoh **stee**-lay
jazz / blues	**jazz / blues**	jahzz / "blues"
singer	**cantante**	kahn-**tahn**-tay
concert	**concerto**	kohn-**chehr**-toh
show	**spettacolo**	spay-**tah**-koh-loh
dancing	**ballare**	bah-**lah**-ray
folk dancing	**danze popolari**	**dahnt**-say poh-poh-**lah**-ree
disco	**discoteca**	dee-skoh-**tay**-kah
no cover charge	**ingresso libero**	een-**gray**-soh **lee**-bay-roh

ENTERTAINMENT

Phoning

Where is the nearest phone?	**Dov'è il telefono più vicino?**	doh-**veh** eel tay-**lay**-foh-noh pew vee-**chee**-noh
I'd like to telephone...	**Vorrei fare una telefonata...**	vor-**rehee** fah-ray **oo**-nah tay-lay-foh-**nah**-tah
...the United States.	**...negli Stati Uniti.**	**nayl**-yee **stah**-tee oo-**nee**-tee
How much per minute?	**Quanto costa al minuto?**	**kwahn**-toh **kos**-tah ahl mee-**noo**-toh
I'd like to make a... call.	**Vorrei fare una telefonata...**	vor-**rehee** fah-ray **oo**-nah tay-lay-foh-**nah**-tah
...local	**...urbana.**	oor-**bah**-nah
...collect	**...a carico dell'utente.**	ah **kah**-ree-koh day-loo-**tehn**-tay
...credit card	**...con la carta di credito.**	kohn lah **kar**-tah dee **kray**-dee-toh
...long distance (within Italy)	**...interurbana.**	een-tay-roor-**bah**-nah
...international	**...internazionale.**	een-tehr-naht-seeoh-**nah**-lay
It doesn't work.	**Non funziona.**	nohn foont-seeoh-nah
May I use your phone?	**Posso usare il telefono?**	**pos**-soh oo-**zah**-ray eel tay-**lay**-foh-noh
Can you dial for me?	**Può fare il numero per me?**	pwoh **fah**-ray eel **noo**-may-roh pehr may
Can you talk for me?	**Può parlare per me?**	pwoh par-**lah**-ray pehr may
It's busy.	**È occupato.**	eh oh-koo-**pah**-toh
Will you try again?	**Può riprovare?**	pwoh ree-proh-**vah**-ray

Hello. (answering the phone)	**Pronto.**	**pron**-toh
My name is...	**Mi chiamo...**	mee kee**ah**-moh
My number is...	**Il mio numero è...**	eel **mee**-oh **noo**-may-roh eh
Speak slowly and clearly.	**Parli lentamente e chiaramente.**	**par**-lee layn-tah-**mayn**-tay ay keeah-rah-**mayn**-tay
Wait a moment.	**Un momento.**	oon moh-**mayn**-toh
Don't hang up.	**Non agganci.**	nohn ah-**gahn**-chee

Key telephone words:

telephone	**telefono**	tay-**lay**-foh-noh
telephone card	**carta telefonica**	**kar**-tah tay-lay-**foh**-nee-kah
operator	**centralinista**	chayn-trah-lee-**nee**-stah
international assistance	**assistenza per chiamate internazionali**	ah-see-**stehnt**-sah pehr keeah-**mah**-tay een-tehr-naht-seeoh-**nah**-lee
country code	**prefisso per il paese**	pray-**fee**-soh pehr eel pah-**ay**-zay
area code	**prefisso**	pray-**fee**-soh
telephone book	**elenco telefonico**	ay-**lehn**-koh tay-lay-**foh**-nee-koh
yellow pages	**pagine gialle**	**pah**-jee-nay **jah**-lay
metered phone	**telefono a scatti**	tay-**lay**-foh-noh ah **skah**-tee
out of service	**guasto**	goo**ah**-stoh

PHONING

Telephoning in Italy can be expensive, and a real headache. When dealing on the phone with someone who only speaks Italian, you might try asking someone to talk for you on your end.

The public phones use coins or a telephone card (*carta telefonica*). These easy-to-use phone cards are sold at post offices, train stations, *tabaccheria* (tobacco shops), and machines near phone booths.

You can call locally or internationally from public phone booths, post offices, and metered phones in cafés and bars. Unless you're using toll-free "USA Direct"-style services, long distance calls from your hotel, as in any country, are a terrible rip-off. For more details, see "Let's Talk Telephones" later in this book.

Mailing

Where is the post office?	**Dov'è la Posta?**	doh-**veh** lah **poh**-stah
Which window for...?	**Qual'è lo sportello per...?**	kwah-**leh** loh spor-**tehl**-loh pehr
...stamps	**...francobolli**	frahn-koh-**boh**-lee
...packages	**...pacchi**	**pah**-kee
To the United States...	**Per Stati Uniti...**	pehr **stah**-tee oo-**nee**-tee
...by air mail.	**...per via aerea.**	pehr **vee**-ah ah-**ay**-ray-ah
...slow and cheap.	**...lento e economico.**	**lehn**-toh ay ay-koh-**noh**-mee-koh
How much is it?	**Quanto costa?**	**kwahn**-toh **kos**-tah
How many days will it take?	**Quanti giorni ci vogliono?**	**kwahn**-tee **jor**-nee chee **vohl**-yoh-noh

Licking the postal code:

Post & Telegraph Office	**Poste e Telegrafi**	**poh**-stah ay tay-**lay**-grah-fee
post office	**ufficio postale**	oo-**fee**-choh poh-**stah**-lay
stamp	**francobollo**	frahn-koh-**boh**-loh
postcard	**cartolina**	kar-toh-**lee**-nah
letter	**lettera**	**leht**-tay-rah
aerogram	**aerogramma**	ah-ay-roh-**grah**-mah
envelope	**busta**	**boo**-stah
package	**pacco**	**pah**-koh

MAILING

box	**scatola**	**skah**-toh-lah
string / tape	**filo / cassetta**	**fee**-loh / kah-**say**-tah
mailbox	**cassetta postale**	kah-**say**-tah poh-**stah**-lay
air mail	**per via aerea**	pehr **vee**-ah ah-**ay**-ray-ah
express	**espresso**	ay-**sprehs**-soh
slow and cheap	**lento e economico**	**lehn**-toh ay ay-koh-**noh**-mee-koh
book rate	**prezzo di listino**	**preht**-soh dee lee-**stee**-noh
weight limit	**limite di peso**	lee-**mee**-tay dee **pay**-zoh
registered	**raccomandata**	rah-koh-mahn-**dah**-tah
insured	**assicurato**	ah-see-koo-**rah**-toh
fragile	**fragile**	frah-**jee**-lay
contents	**contenuto**	kohn-tay-**noo**-toh
customs	**dogana**	doh-**gah**-nah
to / from	**da / a**	dah / ah
address	**indirizzo**	een-dee-**reet**-soh
zip code	**codice postale**	koh-**dee**-chay poh-**stah**-lay
general delivery	**fermo posta**	**fehr**-moh **poh**-stah

In Italy, you can often get stamps at the corner *tabaccheria* (tobacco shop). As long as you know which stamps you need, this is a great convenience. Unless you like to gamble, avoid mailing packages from Italy. The most reliable post offices are in the Vatican City.

Red Tape & Profanity

Filling out Italian forms:

Signore / Signora / Signorina	Mr. / Mrs. / Miss
nome	first name
cognome	name
indirizzo	address
domicilio	address
strada	street
città	city
stato	state
paese	country
nazionalità	nationality
origine / destinazione	origin / destination
età	age
data di nascita	date of birth
luogo di nascita	place of birth
sesso	sex
sposato / sposata	married man / married woman
scapolo / nubile	single man / single woman
professione	profession
adulto	adult
bambino / ragazzo / ragazza	child / boy / girl
bambini	children
famiglia	family
firma	signature

RED TAPE

Italian profanity:

In any country, red tape inspires profanity. In case you're wondering what the more colorful locals are saying...

Damn it.	**Dannazione.**	dah-naht-**seeoh**-nay
Screw it.	**Vai a fa'n culo.**	**vah**ee ah fahn **koo**-loh
Stick it between your teeth.	**Ficcatelo tra i denti.**	fee-kah-**tay**-loh trah ee **dayn**-tee
Go to hell.	**Vai al diavolo.**	**vah**ee ahl deeah-voh-loh
bastard	**bastardo**	bah-**star**-doh
bitch	**cagna**	**kahn**-yah
breasts (colloq.)	**seno**	**say**-noh
penis (colloq.)	**cazzo**	**kaht**-soh
butthole	**stronzo**	**stront**-soh
shit	**merda**	**mehr**-dah
drunk	**ubriaco**	oo-breeah-koh
idiot	**idiota**	ee-deeoh-tah
jerk	**imbecille**	eem-bay-**chee**-lay
stupid	**stupido**	**stoo**-pee-doh
Did someone...?	**Ma qualcuno ha fatto...?**	mah kwahl-**koo**-noh ah **fah**-toh
...burp	**...un rutto**	oon **roo**-toh
...fart	**...una scoreggia**	**oo**-nah skoh-**ray**-jah

Help!

Help!	**Aiuto!**	ah-**yoo**-toh
Help me!	**Aiutatemi!**	ah-yoo-**tah**-tay-mee
Call a doctor!	**Chiamate un dottore!**	keeah-**mah**-tay oon doh-**toh**-ray
ambulance	**ambulanza**	ahm-boo-**lahnt**-sah
accident	**incidente**	een-chee-**dehn**-tay
injured	**ferito**	fay-**ree**-toh
emergency	**emergenza**	ay-mehr-**jehnt**-sah
fire	**fuoco**	**fwoh**-koh
police	**polizia**	poh-leet-**see**-ah
thief	**ladro**	**lah**-droh
pick-pocket	**borsaiolo**	bor-sah-**yoh**-loh
I've been ripped off.	**Sono stato[a] imbrogliato[a].**	**soh**-noh **stah**-toh eem-brohl-**yah**-toh
I've lost my...	**Ho perso il mio...**	oh **pehr**-soh eel **mee**-oh
...passport.	**...passaporto.**	pah-sah-**por**-toh
...ticket.	**...biglietto.**	beel-**yay**-toh
...baggage.	**...bagaglio.**	bah-**gahl**-yoh
...wallet.	**...portafoglio.**	por-tah-**fohl**-yoh
I've lost...	**Ho perso...**	oh **pehr**-soh
...my purse.	**...la mia borsa.**	la **mee**-ah **bor**-sah
...my faith in humankind.	**...la fiducia nel prossimo.**	lah fee-**doo**-chah nayl **pros**-see-moh
I'm lost.	**Mi sono perso[a].**	mee **soh**-noh **pehr**-soh

Help for women:

Leave me alone.	**Mi lasci in pace.**	mee **lah**-shee een **pah**-chay
I *vant* to be alone.	**Voglio stare sola.**	**vohl**-yoh **stah**-ray **soh**-lah
I'm not interested.	**Non sono interessata.**	nohn **soh**-noh een-tay-ray-**sah**-tah
I'm married.	**Sono sposata.**	**soh**-noh spoh-**zah**-tah
I'm a lesbian.	**Sono lesbica.**	**soh**-noh **lehz**-bee-kah
I have a contagious disease.	**Ho una malattia contagiosa.**	oh **oo**-nah mah-lah-**tee**-ah kohn-tah-**joh**-zah
Don't touch me.	**Non mi tocchi.**	nohn mee **toh**-kee
You're disgusting.	**Tu sei disgustoso.**	too **seh**ee dees-goo-**stoh**-zoh
Stop following me.	**La smetta di seguirmi.**	lah **zmay**-tah dee **say**-gweer-mee
This man is bothering me.	**Questo uomo mi importuna.**	**kway**-stoh **woh**-moh mee eem-por-**too**-nah
Enough!	**Basta!**	**bah**-stah
Get lost!	**Sparisca!**	spah-**ree**-skah
Drop dead!	**Crepi!**	**kray**-pee
I'll call the police.	**Chiamo la polizia.**	**keeah**-moh lah poh-leet-**see**-ah

Whenever macho males threaten to make leering a contact sport, local women stroll arm-in-arm or holding hands. Wearing conservative clothes and avoiding smiley eye contact also convey a "don't hustle me" message.

Health

I feel sick.	**Mi sento male.**	mee **sehn**-toh **mah**-lay
I need a doctor...	**Ho bisogno di un dottore...**	oh bee-**zohn**-yoh dee oon doh-**toh**-ray
...who speaks English.	**...che parli inglese.**	kay **par**-lee een-**glay**-zay
It hurts here.	**Fa male qui.**	fah **mah**-lay kwee
I'm allergic to...	**Sono allergico[a]...**	**soh**-noh ah-**lehr**-jee-koh
...penicillin.	**...alla penicillina.**	**ah**-lah pay-nee-chee-**lee**-nah
I am diabetic.	**Ho il diabete.**	oh eel deeah-**bay**-tay
I've missed a period.	**Ha saltato il ciclo mestruale.**	ah sahl-**tah**-toh eel **chee**-kloh may-stroo-**ah**-lay
My male friend has...	**Il mio amico ha...**	eel **mee**-oh ah-**mee**-koh ah
My female friend has...	**La mia amica ha...**	lah **mee**-ah ah-**mee**-kah ah
I have...	**Ho...**	oh
...a burn.	**...un bruciatura.**	oon broo-chah-**too**-rah
...chest pains.	**...dolore al petto.**	doh-**loh**-ray ahl **peht**-toh
...a cold.	**...un raffreddore.**	oon rah-fray-**doh**-ray
...constipation.	**...stitichezza.**	stee-tee-**kayt**-sah
...a cough.	**...la tosse.**	lah **tos**-say
...diarrhea.	**...diarrea.**	dee-ah-**ray**-ah
...dizziness.	**...la testa che gira.**	lah **tehs**-tah kay **jee**-rah
...a fever.	**...la febbre.**	lah **fehb**-bray
...hemorrhoids.	**...le emorroidi.**	lay ay-moh-roh**ee**-dee
...the flu.	**...l'influenza.**	leen-floo-**ehnt**-sah
...the giggles.	**...la ridarella.**	lah ree-dah-**ray**-lah

HEALTH

...hay fever.	...il raffreddore da fieno.	eel rah-fray-**doh**-ray dah fee**ay**-noh
...a headache.	...il mal di testa.	eel mahl dee **tehs**-tah
...high blood pressure.	...la pressione alta.	lah pray-seeoh-nay **ahl**-tah
...indigestion.	...una indigestione.	**oo**-nah een-dee-jay-stee**oh**-nay
...an infection.	...una infezione.	**oo**-nah een-fay-tsee**oh**-nay
...a migraine.	...l'emicrania.	lay-mee-**krah**-nee-ah
...nausea.	...nausea.	**now**-zee-ah
...a rash.	...una infiammazione.	**oo**-nah een-feeah-maht-see**oh**-nay
...a sore throat.	...la gola infiammata.	lah **goh**-lah een-feeah-**mah**-tah
...a stomach ache.	...il mal di stomaco.	eel mahl dee **stom**-ah-koh
...swelling.	...un gonfiore.	oon gohn-fee**oh**-ray
...a toothache.	...mal di denti.	mahl dee **dehn**-tee
...a venereal disease.	...una malattia venerea.	**oo**-nah mah-lah-**tee**-ah vay-nay-**ray**-ah
...worms.	...vermi.	**vehr**-mee
I have body odor.	Io puzzo.	ee**oh** **poot**-soh
Is it serious?	È grave?	eh **grah**-vay

Handy health words:

pain	**dolore**	doh-**loh**-ray
dentist	**dentista**	dayn-**tee**-stah
doctor	**dottore**	doh-**toh**-ray
nurse	**infermiera**	een-fehr-mee**ay**-rah
health insurance	**assicurazione medica**	ah-see-koo-raht-see**oh**-nay **mehd**-ee-kah
hospital	**ospedale**	oh-spay-**dah**-lay
bandage	**cerotti**	chay-**rot**-tee
medicine	**medicina**	may-dee-**chee**-nah
pharmacy	**farmacia**	far-mah-**chee**-ah
prescription	**prescrizione**	pray-skreet-see**oh**-nay
pill	**pillola**	**pee**-loh-lah
aspirin	**aspirina**	ah-spee-**ree**-nah
non-aspirin substitute	**Saridon**	**sah**-ree-dohn
antibiotic	**antibiotici**	ahn-tee-bee**oh**-tee-chee
cold medicine	**medicina per il raffreddore**	may-dee-**chee**-nah pehr eel rah-fray-**doh**-ray
cough drops	**sciroppo per la tosse**	skee-**roh**-poh pehr lah **tos**-say
pain killer	**medicina per il dolore**	may-dee-**chee**-nah pehr eel doh-**loh**-ray
Preparation H	**Preparazione H**	pray-pah-raht-see**oh**-nay **ah**-kah
vitamins	**vitamine**	vee-tah-**mee**-nay

HEALTH

Contacts and glasses:

glasses	**occhiali**	oh-kee**ah**-lee
sunglasses	**occhiali da sole**	oh-kee**ah**-lee dah **soh**-lay
prescription	**prescrizione**	pray-skreet-see**oh**-nay
lenses...	**lenti...**	**lehn**-tee
...soft / hard	**...morbide / dure**	**mor**-bee-day / **doo**-ray
cleaning solution	**soluzione al sapone**	soh-loot-see**oh**-nay ahl sah-**poh**-nay
soaking solution	**solvente**	sohl-**vehn**-tay
I've... a contact lens.	**Ho... una lente a contatto.**	oh... **oo**-nah **lehn**-tay ah kohn-**tah**-toh
...lost	**...perso**	**pehr**-soh
...swallowed	**...inghiottito**	een-goht-**tee**-toh

Toiletries:

comb	**pettine**	pay-**tee**-nay
conditioner	**balsamo**	**bahl**-sah-moh
condoms	**preservativi**	pray-zehr-vah-**tee**-vee
dental floss	**filo interdentale**	**fee**-loh een-tehr-dayn-**tah**-lay
deodorant	**deodorante**	day-oh-doh-**rahn**-tay
hairbrush	**spazzola per capelli**	spaht-**soh**-lah pehr kah-**pehl**-lee
hand lotion	**crema per le mani**	**kray**-mah pehr lay **mah**-nee
lip salve	**burro di cacao**	**boor**-roh dee kah-**kah**-oh
nail clipper	**tagliaunghie**	tahl-yah-**oong**-geeay

razor	**rasoio**	rah-**zoh**-yoh
sanitary napkins	**assorbenti igienici**	ah-sor-**bayn**-tee ee-jay-**nee**-chee
shampoo	**shampoo**	**shahm**-poh
shaving cream	**crema da barba**	**kray**-mah dah **bar**-bah
soap	**sapone**	sah-**poh**-nay
sunscreen	**protezione solare**	proh-tayt-seeoh-nay soh-**lah**-ray
tampons	**assorbenti interni**	ah-sor-**bayn**-tee een-**tehr**-nee
tissues	**fazzoletti di carta**	faht-soh-**leht**-tee dee **kar**-tah
toilet paper	**carta igienica**	**kar**-tah ee-**jay**-nee-kah
toothbrush	**spazzolino da denti**	spaht-soh-**lee**-noh dah **dayn**-tee
toothpaste	**dentifricio**	dayn-tee-**free**-choh
tweezers	**pinzette**	peent-**say**-tay

HEALTH

Chatting

My name is...	**Mi chiamo...**	mee keeah-moh
What's your name?	**Come si chiama?**	koh-may see keeah-mah
How are you?	**Come sta?**	koh-may stah
Very well, thank you.	**Molto bene, grazie.**	mohl-toh behn-ay graht-seeay
Where are you from?	**Di dove è?**	dee doh-vay eh
What... are you from?	**Da che... viene?**	dah kay... veeay-nay
...city	**...città**	chee-tah
...country	**...paese**	pah-ay-zay
...planet	**...pianeta**	peeah-nay-tah
I'm...	**Sono...**	soh-noh
...American.	**...Americano[a].**	ah-may-ree-kah-noh
...Canadian.	**...Canadese.**	kah-nah-day-zay

Nothing more than feelings:

I am / You are...	**Sono / È...**	soh-noh / eh
...happy.	**...felice.**	fay-lee-chay
...sad.	**...triste.**	tree-stay
...tired.	**...stanco[a].**	stahn-koh
...lucky.	**...fortunato[a].**	for-too-nah-toh
I am / You are...	**Ho / Ha...**	oh / ah
...hungry / thirsty.	**...fame / sete.**	fah-may / say-tay
...homesick.	**...nostalgia.**	noh-stahl-jah
...cold.	**...freddo.**	fray-doh
...too warm.	**...troppo caldo.**	trop-poh kahl-doh

Who's who:

My...	Mio / Mia...	**mee**-oh / **mee**-ah
...male friend / female friend.	...**amico / amica.**	ah-**mee**-koh / ah-**mee**-kah
...boyfriend / girlfriend.	...**ragazzo / ragazza.**	rah-**gaht**-soh / rah-**gaht**-sah
...husband / wife.	...**marito / moglie.**	mah-**ree**-toh / **mohl**-yay
...son / daughter.	...**figlio / figlia.**	**feel**-yoh / **feel**-yah
...brother / sister.	...**fratello / sorella.**	frah-**tehl**-loh / soh-**rehl**-lah
...father / mother.	...**padre / madre.**	**pah**-dray / **mah**-dray
...uncle / aunt.	...**zio / zia.**	**tsee**oh / **tsee**ah
...nephew or niece.	...**nipote.**	nee-**poh**-tay
...male / female cousin.	...**cugino / cugina.**	koo-**gee**-noh / koo-**gee**-nah
...grandfather / grandmother.	...**nonno / nonna.**	**noh**-noh / **noh**-nah
...grandchild.	...**nipote.**	nee-**poh**-tay

Family, school and work:

Are you married? (asked of a woman)	**È sposata?**	eh spoh-**zah**-tah
Are you married? (asked of a man)	**È sposato?**	eh spoh-**zah**-toh
Do you have children?	**Ha bambini?**	ah bahm-**bee**-nee
How many boys and girls?	**Quanti ragazzi e ragazze?**	**kwahn**-tee rah-**gaht**-zee ay rah-**gaht**-zay
Do you have photos?	**Ha foto?**	ah **foh**-toh

How old is your child?	**Quanti anni ha il suo bambino?**	kwahn-tee **ahn**-nee ah eel **soo**-oh bahm-**bee**-noh
Beautiful child!	**Bel bambino!**	behl bahm-**bee**-noh
Beautiful children!	**Bei bambini!**	**beh**ee bahm-**bee**-nee
What are you studying?	**Che cosa sta studiando?**	kay **koh**-zah stah stoo-deeahn-doh
I'm studying...	**Sto studiando...**	stoh stoo-dee**ahn**-doh
I'm... years old.	**Ho... anni.**	oh... **ahn**-nee
How old are you?	**Quanti anni ha?**	kwahn-tee **ahn**-nee ah
Do you have brothers and sisters?	**Ha fratelli e sorelle?**	ah frah-**tehl**-lee ay soh-**rehl**-lay
Will you teach me a simple Italian song?	**Mi insegna una canzone italiana facile?**	mee een-**sayn**-yah **oo**-nah kahnt-**soh**-nay ee-tah-lee**ah**-nah fah-**chee**-lay
I'm a...	**Sono...**	**soh**-noh
...male student / female student.	**...studente / studentessa.**	stoo-**dehn**-tay / stoo-dehn-**tehs**-sah
...teacher.	**...insegnante.**	een-sayn-**yahn**-tay
...worker.	**...operaio[a].**	oh-pay-**rah**-yoh
...bureaucrat.	**...burocrate.**	boo-roh-**kray**-tay
...brain surgeon.	**...chirurgo del cervello.**	kee-**roor**-goh dayl chehr-**vehl**-loh
...professional traveler.	**...turista di professione.**	too-**ree**-stah dee proh-fay-see**oh**-nay
What is your job?	**Che lavoro fa?**	kay lah-**voh**-roh fah
Do you like your work?	**Le piace il suo lavoro?**	lay peeah-chay eel **soo**-oh lah-**voh**-roh

Favorite things:

What... do you like?	**Qual'è il suo... preferito?**	kwah-**leh** eel **soo**-oh... pray-fay-**ree**-toh
...art	**...genere d'arte**	**jay**-nay-ray dar-**tay**
...books	**...genere di libri**	**jay**-nay-ray dee **lee**-bree
...hobby	**...passatempo**	pah-sah-**tehm**-poh
...ice cream	**...gelato**	jay-**lah**-toh
...movie	**...film**	feelm
...male movie star	**...attore**	ah-**toh**-ray
...music	**...genere di musica**	**jay**-nay-ray dee **moo**-zee-kah
...male singer	**...cantante**	kahn-**tahn**-tay
...sport	**...sport**	sport
...vice	**...vizio**	**veet**-seeoh
What... do you like?	**Qual'è la sua... preferita?**	kwah-**leh** lah **soo**-ah... pray-fay-**ree**-tah
...female movie star	**...attrice**	ah-**tree**-chay
...female singer	**...cantante**	kahn-**tahn**-tay

Responses for all occasions:

I like that.	**Mi piace.**	mee pee**ah**-chay
I like you.	**Lei mi piace.**	**leh**ee mee pee**ah**-chay
Great!	**Ottimo!**	**ot**-tee-moh
Perfect.	**Perfetto.**	pehr-**feht**-toh
Funny.	**Divertente.**	dee-vehr-**tehn**-tay
Interesting.	**Interessante.**	een-tay-ray-**sahn**-tay

I don't smoke.	**Non fumo.**	nohn **foo**-moh
Really?	**Davvero?**	dah-**vay**-roh
Congratulations!	**Congratulazioni!**	kohn-grah-too-laht-see**oh**-nee
Well done!	**Bravo[a]!**	**brah**-voh
You're welcome.	**Prego.**	**pray**-goh
Bless you! (after sneeze)	**Salute!**	sah-**loo**-tay
Excuse me.	**Mi scusi.**	mee **skoo**-zee
What a pity.	**Che peccato.**	kay pay-**kah**-toh
That's life.	**Quella è vita.**	**kway**-lah eh **vee**-tah
No problem.	**Non c'è problema.**	nohn cheh proh-**blay**-mah
O.K.	**Va bene.**	vah **behn**-ay
I feel like a pope! (happy)	**Sto come un papa!**	stoh **koh**-may oon **pah**-pah
This is the good life!	**Questa è vita!**	**kway**-stah eh **vee**-tah
Have a good day!	**Buon giornata!**	bwohn jor-**nah**-tah
Good luck!	**Buona fortuna!**	**bwoh**-nah for-**too**-nah
Let's go!	**Andiamo!**	ahn-dee**ah**-moh

Thanks a million:

A thousand thanks.	**Grazie mille.**	**graht**-seeay **mee**-lay
You are...	**Lei è...**	**leh**ee eh
...kind.	**...gentile.**	jayn-**tee**-lay
...helpful.	**...di aiuto.**	dee ah-**yoo**-toh
...generous.	**...generoso[a].**	jay-nay-**roh**-zoh
...hairy.	**...peloso[a].**	pay-**loh**-zoh

It's / You are...	È / Lei è...	eh / **leh**ee eh
...great.	...ottimo.	**ot**-tee-moh
...great fun.	...un vero divertimento.	oon **vay**-roh dee-vehr-tee-**mayn**-toh
You've gone to much trouble.	Si è veramente disturbato[a].	see eh vay-rah-**mayn**-tay dee-stoor-**bah**-toh
You are a saint.	Lei è un santo[a].	**leh**ee eh oon **sahn**-toh
I will remember you...	Mi ricorderò di Lei...	mee ree-kor-day-**roh** dee **leh**ee
...always.	...sempre.	**sehm**-pray
...till Tuesday.	...fino a martedì.	**fee**-noh ah mar-tay-**dee**

Travel talk:

I am / Are you...?	Sono / È...?	**soh**-noh / eh
...on vacation	...in vacanza	een vah-**kahnt**-sah
...on business	...qui per lavoro	kwee pehr lah-**voh**-roh
How long have you been traveling?	Da quanto tempo è in viaggio?	dah **kwahn**-toh **tehm**-poh eh een vee**ah**-joh
day / week	giorno / settimana	**jor**-noh / say-tee-**mah**-nah
month / year	mese / anno	**may**-zay / **ahn**-noh
When are you going home?	Quando ritorna a casa?	**kwahn**-doh ree-**tor**-nah ah **kah**-zah
This is my first time in...	Questa è la mia prima volta in...	**kway**-stah eh lah **mee**-ah **pree**-mah **vohl**-tah een
It is (not) a tourist trap.	(Non) è una trappola per turisti.	(nohn) eh **oo**-nah trah-**poh**-lah pehr too-**ree**-stee
I'm happy here.	Sono felice qui.	**soh**-noh fay-**lee**-chay kwee

The Italians are friendly.	**Gli italiani sono amichevoli.**	**lee**yee ee-tah-leeah-nee **soh**-noh ah-mee-kay-**voh**-lee
Italy is fantastic.	**L'Italia è fantastica.**	lee-**tahl**-yah eh fahn-**tah**-stee-koh
Travel is good for your health.	**Viaggiare fa bene alla salute.**	veeah-**jah**-ray fah **behn**-ay **ah**-lah sah-**loo**-tay
Have a good trip!	**Buon viaggio!**	bwohn veeah-**joh**

Map musings:

These phrases and the maps on the following pages will help you delve into family history.

I live here.	**Abito qui.**	ah-**bee**-toh kwee
I was born here.	**Sono nato[a] qui.**	**soh**-noh **nah**-toh kwee
My ancestors came from...	**I miei antenati vennero da...**	ee mee**ay**-ee ahn-tay-**nah**-tee vay-**nay**-roh dah
I've traveled to...	**Sono stato[a] a...**	**soh**-noh **stah**-toh ah
Next I'll go to...	**Poi andrò a...**	**poh**ee ahn-**droh** ah
Where do you live?	**Dove abita?**	**doh**-vay ah-**bee**-tah
Where were you born?	**Dove è nato[a]?**	**doh**-vay eh **nah**-toh
Where did your ancestors come from?	**Da dove vennero i suoi antenati?**	dah **doh**-vay vay-**nay**-roh ee **swoh**-ee ahn-tay-**nah**-tee
Where have you traveled?	**Dove è stato[a]?**	**doh**-vay eh **stah**-toh
Where are you going?	**Dove va?**	**doh**-vay vah
Where would you like to go?	**Dove vorrebbe andare?**	**doh**-vay voh-**ray**-bay ahn-**dah**-ray

Italy

Create Your Own Conversation

Mix and match these words into a conversation, and make
it as deep or silly as you want.

Who:

I / you	**io / Lei**	**ee**oh / **leh**ee
he / she	**lui / lei**	lwee / **leh**ee
we / they	**noi / loro**	**noh**ee / **loh**-roh
my / your...	**mio / suo...**	**mee**-oh / **soo**-oh
...parents / children	**...genitori / figli**	jay-nee-**toh**-ree / **feel**-yee
men / women	**uomini / donne**	woh-**mee**-nee / **don**-nay
rich / poor	**ricchi / poveri**	**ree**-kee / **poh**-vay-ree
politicians	**politici**	poh-**lee**-tee-chee
big business	**grande attività**	**grahn**-day ah-tee-vee-**tah**
mafia	**mafia**	**mah**-feeah
military	**militare**	mee-lee-**tah**-ray
the Italians	**gli italiani**	leeyee ee-tah-leeah-nee
the French	**i francesi**	ee frahn-**chay**-zee
the Germans	**i tedeschi**	ee tay-**dehs**-kee
the Americans	**gli americani**	leeyee ah-may-ree-**kah**-nee
liberals	**liberali**	lee-bay-**rah**-lee
conservatives	**conservatori**	kohn-sehr-vah-**toh**-ree
radicals	**radicali**	rah-dee-**kah**-lee
travelers	**viaggiatori**	veeah-jah-**toh**-ree
everyone	**tutti**	**too**-tee
God	**Dio**	**dee**oh

What:

want	**volere**	voh-**lay**-ray
need	**aver bisogno**	ah-vehr bee-**zohn**-yoh
take / give	**prendere / dare**	**prehn**-day-ray / **dah**-ray
love / hate	**amare / odiare**	ah-**mah**-ray / oh-deeah-ray
work / play	**lavorare / giocare**	lah-voh-**rah**-ray / joh-**kah**-ray
have / lack	**avere / non avere**	ah-**vay**-ray / nohn ah-**vay**-ray
learn / fear	**imparare / temere**	eem-pah-**rah**-ray / tay-**may**-ray
help / abuse	**aiutare / abusare**	ah-yoo-**tah**-ray / ah-boo-**zah**-ray
prosper / suffer	**prosperare / soffrire**	proh-spay-**rah**-ray / soh-**free**-ray
buy / sell	**comprare / vendere**	kohm-**prah**-ray / vayn-**day**-ray

Why:

love / sex	**amore / sesso**	ah-**moh**-ray / **sehs**-soh
money	**denaro**	day-**nah**-roh
power	**potere**	poh-**tay**-ray
work	**lavoro**	lah-**voh**-roh
food	**cibo**	**chee**-boh
family	**famiglia**	fah-**meel**-yah
health	**salute**	sah-**loo**-tay
hope	**speranza**	spay-**rahnt**-sah
education	**educazione**	ay-doo-kaht-see**oh**-nay
guns	**armi**	**ar**-mee
religion	**religione**	ray-lee-**joh**-nay
happiness	**felicità**	fay-lee-chee-**tah**

marijuana	**marijuana**	mah-ree-**wahn**-nah
democracy	**democrazia**	day-moh-kraht-**see**-ah
taxes	**tasse**	**tah**-say
lies	**bugie**	boo-**jee**-ay
corruption	**corruzione**	kor-root-seeoh-nay
pollution	**inquinamento**	een-kwee-nah-**mayn**-toh
television	**televisione**	tay-lay-vee-zeeoh-nay
relaxation	**rilassamento**	ree-lah-sah-**mayn**-toh
violence	**violenza**	vee-oh-**lehnt**-sah
racism	**razzismo**	raht-**seez**-moh
respect	**rispetto**	ree-**spay**-toh
war / peace	**guerra / pace**	**gwehr**-rah / **pah**-chay
global perspective	**prospettiva globale**	proh-spay-**tee**-vah gloh-**bah**-lay

You be the judge:

(no) problem	**(non c'è) problema**	(nohn chay) proh-**blay**-mah
(not) good	**(non) bene**	(nohn) **behn**-ay
(not) dangerous	**(non) pericoloso**	(nohn) pay-ree-koh-**loh**-zoh
(not) fair	**(non) giusto**	(nohn) **joo**-stoh
(not) guilty	**(non) colpevole**	(nohn) kohl-pay-**voh**-lay
(not) powerful	**(non) potente**	(nohn) poh-**tehn**-tay
(not) stupid	**(non) stupido**	(nohn) **stoo**-pee-doh
(not) happy	**(non) felice**	(nohn) fay-**lee**-chay
because / for	**perchè / per**	pehr-**keh** / pehr
and / or / from	**e / o / da**	ay / oh / dah

too much	**troppo**	**trop**-poh
enough	**abbastanza**	ah-bah-**stahnt**-sah
never enough	**mai abbastanza**	**mah**ee ah-bah-**stahnt**-sah
worse / better	**peggio / meglio**	**peh**-joh / **mehl**-yoh
same	**stesso**	**stay**-soh
here / everywhere	**qui / ovunque**	kwee / oh-**voon**-kway

Assorted beginnings and endings:

I like...	**Mi piace...**	mee pee**ah**-chay
I don't like...	**Non mi piace...**	nohn mee pee**ah**-chay
Do you like...?	**Le piace...?**	lay pee**ah**-chay
When I was young...	**Quando ero più giovane...**	**kwahn**-doh **ay**-roh pew joh-**vah**-nay
I am / Are you...?	**Sono / È...?**	**soh**-noh / eh
...an optimist / pessimist	**...ottimista / pessimista**	ot-tee-**mee**-stah / pay-see-**mee**-stah
I believe...	**Credo...**	**kray**-doh
I don't believe...	**Non credo...**	nohn **kray**-doh
Do you believe...?	**Lei crede...?**	**leh**ee **kray**-day
...in God	**...in Dio**	een **dee**oh
...in life after death	**...nella vita ultraterrena**	**nay**-lah **vee**-tah ool-trah-tay-**ray**-nah
...in extraterrestrial life	**...negli extraterrestri**	**nayl**-yee ehk-strah-tehr-**rehs**-tree
...in Santa Claus	**...in Babbo Natale**	een **bah**-boh nah-**tah**-lay
Yes. / No.	**Si. / No.**	see / noh

Maybe. / I don't know.	**Forse. / Non lo so.**	**for**-say / nohn loh soh
What's most important in life?	**Qual'è la cosa più importante nella vita?**	kwah-**leh** lah **koh**-zah pew eem-por-**tahn**-tay **nay**-lah **vee**-tah
The problem is...	**Il problema è...**	eel proh-**blay**-mah eh
The answer is...	**La risposta è...**	lah ree-**spoh**-stah eh
We have solved the world's problems.	**Abbiamo risolto i problemi del mondo.**	ah-beeah-moh ree-**zohl**-toh ee proh-**blay**-mee dayl **mohn**-doh

Weather:

What's the weather tomorrow?	**Come sarà il tempo domani?**	**koh**-may sah-**rah** eel **tehm**-poh doh-**mah**-nee
sunny / cloudy	**bello / nuvoloso**	**behl**-loh / noo-voh-**loh**-zoh
hot / cold	**caldo / freddo**	**kahl**-doh / **fray**-doh
muggy / windy	**umido / ventoso**	oo-**mee**-doh / vehn-**toh**-zoh
rain / snow	**pioggia / neve**	peeoh-jah / **nay**-vay

An Italian Romance

Words of love:

I / me / you	**Io / mi / ti**	**ee**oh / mee / tee
flirt	**flirtare**	fleer-**tah**-ray
kiss	**bacio**	**bah**-choh
hug	**abbraccio**	ah-**brah**-choh
love	**amore**	ah-**moh**-ray
make love	**fare l'amore**	**fah**-ray lah-**moh**-ray
condom	**preservativo**	pray-zehr-vah-**tee**-voh
contraceptive	**contraccetivo**	kohn-trah-chay-**tee**-voh
safe sex	**sesso prudente**	**sehs**-soh proo-**dehn**-tay
sexy	**sensuale**	sayn-soo**ah**-lay
cozy	**accogliente**	ah-kohl-**yehn**-tay
romantic	**romantico**	roh-**mahn**-tee-koh
honey bunch	**dolce come il miele**	**dohl**-chay **koh**-may eel mee**ay**-lay
cupcake	**pasticcino**	pah-stee-**chee**-noh
sugar pie	**zuccherino**	tsoo-kay-**ree**-noh
pussy cat	**gattino**	gah-**tee**-noh

Ah, amore:

What's the matter?	**Qual'è il problema?**	kwah-**leh** eel proh-**blay**-mah
Nothing.	**Niente.**	nee**ehn**-tay

I am / Are you...?	Sono / È...?	**soh**-noh / eh
...straight	...normale	nor-**mah**-lay
...gay	...gay	gay
...undecided	...indeciso[a]	een-day-**chee**-zoh
...prudish	...pudico[a]	**poo**-dee-koh
...horny	...allupato[a]	ah-loo-**pah**-toh
We are on our honeymoon.	Siamo in luna di miele.	seeah-moh een **loo**-nah dee meeay-lay
I have a boy friend / a girl friend.	Ho il ragazzo / la ragazza.	oh eel rah-**gaht**-soh / lah rah-**gaht**-sah
I'm married.	Sono sposato[a].	**soh**-noh spoh-**zah**-toh
I'm not married.	Non sono sposato[a].	nohn **soh**-noh spoh-**zah**-toh
I'm rich and single.	Sono ricco[a] e singolo[a].	**soh**-noh **ree**-koh ay **seeng**-goh-loh
I'm lonely.	Sono solo[a].	**soh**-noh **soh**-loh
I have no diseases.	Non ho malattie.	nohn oh mah-lah-**tee**-ay
I have many diseases.	Ho molte malattie.	oh **mohl**-tay mah-lah-**tee**-ay
Can I see you again?	Ti posso rivedere?	tee **pos**-soh ree-vay-**day**-ray
You are my most beautiful souvenir.	Sei il mio più bel ricordo.	sehee eel **mee**-oh pew behl ree-**kor**-doh
Is this an aphrodisiac?	È un afrodisiaco questo?	eh oon ah-froh-dee-**zee**-ah-koh **kway**-stoh
This is (not) my first time.	Questa (non) è la mia prima volta.	**kway**-stah (nohn) eh lah **mee**-ah **pree**-mah **vohl**-tah
Do you do this often?	Lo fai spesso?	loh **fahee spay**-soh
How's my breath?	Com'è il mio fiato?	koh-**meh** eel **mee**-oh feeah-toh

CHATTING

Let's just be friends.	**Solo amici.**	**soh**-loh ah-**mee**-chee
I'll pay for my share.	**Pago per la mia parte.**	**pah**-goh pehr lah **mee**-ah **par**-tay
Would you like a massage...?	**Vorresti un massaggio...?**	vor-**ray**-stee oon mah-**sah**-joh
...for your back	**...alla schiena**	ah-lah sheeay-nah
...for your feet	**....ai piedi**	ahee peeay-dee
Why not?	**Perchè no?**	pehr-**keh** noh
Try it.	**Provalo.**	**proh**-vah-loh
It tickles.	**Fa il solletico.**	fah eel soh-**lay**-tee-koh
Oh my God.	**Oh mio Dio.**	oh **mee**-oh **dee**-oh
I love you.	**Ti amo.**	tee **ah**-moh
Darling, will you marry me?	**Cara, mi vuoi sposare?**	**kah**-rah mee **vwoh**ee spoh-**zah**-ray

Conversing with Italian animals:

rooster / cock-a-doodle-doo	**gallo / chicchirichì**	**gah**-loh / kee-kee-ree-**kee**
bird / tweet tweet	**uccello / cip cip**	oo-**chehl**-loh / cheep cheep
cat / meow	**gatto / miao**	**gah**-toh / **mee**-ow
dog / bark bark	**cane / bau bau**	**kah**-nay / bow bow
duck / quack quack	**oca / quac quac**	**oh**-kah / kwahk kwahk
cow / moo	**mucca / muu**	**moo**-kah / moo
pig / oink oink	**maiale / oinc oinc**	mah-**yah**-lay / oynk oynk

English-Italian Dictionary

You'll see some of the words in the dictionary listed like this: aggressivo[a]. Use the *a* ending (prounounced "ah") if you're talking about a woman.

A

above sopra
accident incidente
accountant commercialista
adaptor adattatore
address indirizzo
adult adulto
afraid spaventato[a]
after dopo
afternoon pomeriggio
aftershave dopobarba
afterwards più tardi
again ancora
age età
aggressive aggressivo[a]
agree d'accordo
AIDS AIDS
air aria
air-conditioned aria condizionata
airline aeroplano
air mail via aerea
airport aeroporto
alarm clock sveglia
alcohol alcool
allergic allergico[a]

allergies allergie
alone solo[a]
already già
always sempre
ancestor antenato[a]
ancient antico
and e
angry arrabbiato[a]
ankle caviglia
animal animale
another un altro
answer risposta
antibiotic antibiotico
antiques antichità
apartment appartamento
apology scuse
appetizers antipasti
apple mela
appointment appuntamento
approximately più o meno
arrivals arrivi
arrive arrivare
arm braccio
art arte
artificial artificiale
artist artista

ashtray portacenere
ask domandare
aspirin aspirina
at a
attractive bello[a]
aunt zia
Austria Austria
autumn autunno

B

baby bambino[a]
babysitter bambinaia
backpack zainetto
bad cattivo
bag sacchetto
baggage bagaglio
bakery panificio
balcony balcone
ball palla
banana banana
band-aid cerotto
bank banca
barber barbiere
basement seminterrato
basket cestino
bath bagno
bathroom bagno
bathtub vasca da bagno
battery batteria
beach spiaggia
beard barba

beautiful bello[a]
because perchè
bed letto
bedroom camera da letto
bedsheet lenzuolo
beef manzo
beer birra
before prima
begin cominciare
behind dietro
below sotto
belt cintura
best il migliore
better meglio
bib bavaglino
bicycle bicicletta
big grande
bill (payment) conto
bird uccello
birthday compleanno
bite (n) morso
black nero
blanket coperta
blond biondo[a]
blood sangue
blouse camicetta
blue blu
boat barca
body corpo
boiled bollito
bomb bomba
book libro
book shop libreria

boots stivali
border frontiera
borrow prendere in prestito
boss capo
bottle bottiglia
bottom fondo
bowl boccia
box scatola
boy ragazzo
bra reggiseno
bracelet braccialetto
bread pane
breakfast colazione
bridge ponte
briefs mutandoni
Britain Britannia
broken rotto
brother fratello
brown marrone
bucket secchio
building edificio
bulb bulbo
burn (n) bruciatura
bus autobus
business affari
button bottone
buy comprare
by (via) in

C

calendar calendario
calorie calorie
camera macchina fotografica
camping campeggio
can (n) lattina
can (v) potere
Canada Canada
can opener apriscatola
canal canale
candle candela
candy caramella
canoe canoa
cap berretto
captain capitano
car macchina
carafe caraffa
card cartina
cards (deck) carte
careful prudente
carpet tappeto
carry portare
cashier cassiere
cassette cassetta
castle castello
cat gatto
catch (v) prendere
cathedral cattedrale
cave grotta
cellar cantina
center centro
century secolo

chair sedia
change (n) cambio
change (v) cambiare
charming affascinante
cheap economico
check assegno
Cheers! Salute!
cheese formaggio
chicken pollo
children bambini
Chinese (adj) cinese
chocolate cioccolato
Christmas Natale
church chiesa
cigarette sigarette
cinema cinema
city città
class classe
clean (adj) pulito
clear chiaro
cliff dirupo
closed chiuso
cloth stoffa
clothes vestiti
clothesline marca
clothes pins spilla
cloudy nuvoloso
coast costa
coat hanger appendiabiti
coffee caffè
coins monete
cold (adj) freddo
colors colori

comb (n) pettine
come venire
comfortable confortevole
compact disc compact disc
complain protestare
complicated complicato
computer computer
concert concerto
condom preservativo
conductor conduttore
confirm confermare
congratulations congratulazioni
connection (train) coincidenza
constipation stitichezza
cook (v) cucinare
cool fresco
cork tappo
corkscrew cavatappi
corner angolo
corridor corridoio
cost (v) costare
cot lettino
cotton cotone
cough (v) tossire
cough drop sciroppo
country paese
countryside campagna
cousin cugino[a]
cow mucca
cozy confortevole
crafts arte
cream panna
credit card carta di credito

crowd (n) folla
cry (v) piangere
cup tazza

D

dad papà
dance (v) ballare
danger pericolo
dangerous pericoloso
dark scuro
daughter figlia
day giorno
dead morto
delay ritardo
delicious delizioso
dental floss filo interdentale
dentist dentista
deodorant deodorante
depart partire
departures partenze
deposit deposito
dessert dolci
detour deviazione
diabetic diabetico[a]
diamond diamante
diaper pannolino
diarrhea diarrea
dictionary dizionario
die morire
difficult difficile
dinner cena

direct diretto
direction direzione
dirty sporco
discount sconto
disease malattia
disturb disturbare
divorced divorziato[a]
doctor dottore
dog cane
doll bambola
donkey asino
door porta
dormitory camerata
double doppio
down giù
dream (n) sogno
dream (v) sognare
dress (n) vestito
drink (n) bevanda
drive (v) guidare
driver autista
drunk ubriaco
dry secco, asciutto

E

each ogni
ear orecchio
early presto
earplugs tappi per le orecchie
earrings orecchini
earth terra

east est
Easter Pasqua
easy facile
eat mangiare
elbow gomito
elevator ascensore
embarrassing imbarazzante
embassy ambasciata
empty vuoto
engineer ingeniere
English inglese
enjoy divertirsi
enough abbastanza
entrance ingresso
entry entrata
envelope busta
eraser gomma da cancellare
especially specialmente
Europe Europa
evening sera
every ogni
everything tutto
exactly esattamente
example esempio
excellent eccellente
except eccetto
exchange (n) cambio
excuse me mi scusi
exhausted esausto
exit uscita
expensive caro
explain spiegare
eye occhio

F

face faccia
factory fabbrica
fall (v) cadere
false falso
family famiglia
famous famoso[a]
fantastic fantastico[a]
far lontano
farm fattoria
farmer contadino[a]
fashion moda
fat (adj) grasso[a]
father padre
faucet rubinetto
fax fax
female femmina
ferry traghetto
fever febbre
few poco
field campo
fight (n) lotta
fight (v) combattere
fine (good) bene
finger dito
finish (v) finire
fireworks fuochi d'artificio
first primo
first aid primo soccorso
first class prima classe
fish pesce
fish (v) pescare

fix (v) aggiustare
fizzy frizzante
flag bandiera
flashlight torcia
flavor (n) aroma
flea pulce
flight volo
flower fiore
flu influenza
fly volare
fog nebbia
food cibo
foot piede
football calcio
for per
forbidden vietato
foreign straniero
forget dimenticare
fork forchetta
fountain fontana
France Francia
free (no cost) gratis
fresh fresco
Friday venerdì
friend amico
friendship amicizia
frisbee frisbee
from da
fruit frutta
fun divertimento
funeral funerale
funny divertente
furniture mobili

future futuro

G

gallery galleria
game gioco
garage garage
garden giardino
gardening giardinaggio
gas benzina
gas station benzinaio
gay omosessuale
gentleman signore
genuine genuino
Germany Germania
gift regalo
girl ragazza
give dare
glass bicchiere
glasses (eye) occhiali
gloves guanti
go andare
God Dio
gold oro
golf golf
good buono
goodbye arrivederci
good day buon giorno
go through attraversare
grammar grammatica
grandchild nipote
grandfather nonno
grandmother nonna

gray grigio
greasy grasso
great ottimo
Greece Grecia
green verde
grocery store alimentari
guarantee garantito
guest ospite
guide guida
guidebook guida
guitar chitarra
gum gomma da masticare
gun pistola

H

hair capelli
haircut taglio di capelli
hand mano
handicapped andicappato
handicrafts artigianato
handle (n) manico
handsome attraente
happy contento[a]
harbor porto
hard duro
hat cappello
hate (v) odiare
have avere
he lui
head testa
headache mal di testa
healthy sano

hear udire
heart cuore
heat (n) calore
heat (v) scaldare
heaven paradiso
heavy pesante
hello ciao
help (n) aiuto
help aiutare
hemorrhoids emorroidi
here qui
hi ciao
high alto
highchair seggiolone
highway autostrada
hike fare una gita
hill collina
history storia
hitchhike autostop
hobby hobby
hole buco
holiday giorno festivo
homemade casalingo
homesick nostalgico[a]
honest onesto[a]
honeymoon luna di miele
horrible orribile
horse cavallo
horse riding equitazione
hospital ospedale
hot caldo
hotel hotel
hour ora

house casa
how many quanti
how much ($) quanto costa
how come
hungry affamato
hurry (v) avere fretta
husband marito
hydrofoil aliscafo

I

I io
ice ghiaccio
ice cream gelato
ill malato[a]
immediately immediatamente
important importante
imported importato
impossible impossibile
in in
included incluso
incredible incredibile
independent indipendente
indigestion indigestione
industry industria
information informazioni
injured infortunato
innocent innocente
insect insetto
insect repellant lozione anti-zanzare
inside dentro
instant istante

instead invece
insurance assicurazione
intelligent intelligente
interesting interessante
invitation invito
iodine iodio
is è
island isola
Italy Italia
itch (n) prurito

J

jacket giubbotto
jaw mascella
jeans jeans
jewelry gioielleria
job lavoro
jogging footing
joke (n) scherzo
journey viaggio
juice succo
jump (v) saltare

K

keep tenere
kettle bollitore
key chiave
kill uccidere
kind gentile
king re
kiss bacio

kitchen cucina
knee ginocchio
knife coltello
know sapere

L

ladder scala
ladies signore
lake lago
lamb agnello
language lingua
large grande
last ultimo
late tardi
later più tardi
laugh (v) ridere
laundromat lavanderia
lawyer avvocato
lazy pigro[a]
leather pelle
leave partire
left sinistra
leg gamba
lend prestare
letter lettera
library biblioteca
life vita
light (n) luce
light bulb lampadina
lighter (n) accendino
like (v) piacere
lip labbro

list lista
listen ascoltare
liter litro
little (adj) piccolo
live (v) vivere
local locale
lock (v) chiudere
lock (n) serratura
lockers armadietti
look guardare
lost perso[a]
loud forte
love (v) amare
lover amante
low basso
lozenges pastiglie per la gola
luck fortuna
luggage bagaglio
lukewarm tiepido
lungs polmoni

M

macho macho
mad arrabbiato[a]
magazine rivista
mail (n) posta
main principale
make (v) fare
male maschio
man uomo
manager direttore
many molti

map cartina
market mercato
married sposato[a]
matches fiammiferi
maximum massimo
maybe forse
meat carne
medicine medicina
medium medio
men uomini
menu menù
message messaggio
metal metallo
midnight mezzanotte
mineral water acqua minerale
minimum minimo
minutes minuti
mirror specchio
Miss Signorina
mistake errore
misunderstanding
 incomprensione
mix (n) misto
modern moderno
moment momento
Monday lunedì
money soldi
month mese
monument monumento
moon luna
more ancora
morning mattina
mosquito zanzara

mother madre
mother-in-law suocera
mountain montagna
moustache baffi
mouth bocca
movie film
Mr. Signore
Mrs. Signora
much molto
muscle muscolo
museum museo
music musica
my mio / mia

N

nail clipper tagliaunghie
naked nudo[a]
name nome
napkin salvietta
narrow stretto
nationality nazionalità
natural naturale
nature natura
nausea nausea
near vicino
necessary necessario
necklace collana
need avere bisogno di
needle ago
nephew nipote
nervous nervoso[a]
never mai

DICTIONARY

new nuovo
newspaper giornale
next prossimo
nice bello[a]
niece nipote
nickname soprannome
night notte
no no
noisy rumoroso[a]
non-smoking vietato fumare
noon mezzogiorno
normal normale
north nord
nose naso
not non
notebook blocco note
nothing niente
no vacancy completo
now adesso

O

occupation lavoro
occupied occupato
ocean oceano
of di
office ufficio
oil (n) olio
OK d'accordo
old vecchio[a]
on su
once una volta
one way (street) senso unico

one way (ticket) andata
only solo
open (adj) aperto
open (v) aprire
opera opera
operator centralinista
optician ottico
or o
orange (color) arancione
orange (fruit) arancia
original originale
other altro
outdoors all'aria aperta
oven forno
over (finished) finito
own (v) possedere
owner padrone

P

pacifier succhiotto
package pacco
page pagina
pail secchio
pain dolore
painting quadro
palace palazzo
panties mutande
pants pantaloni
paper carta
paper clip graffetta
parents genitori
park (v) parcheggiare

park (garden) parco
party festa
passenger passeggero[a]
passport passaporto
pay pagare
peace pace
pedestrian pedone
pen penna
pencil matita
people persone
pepper pepe
percent percentuale
perfect perfetto
perfume profumo
period (of time) periodo
period (woman's) mestruazioni
person persona
pet (n) animale domestico
pharmacy farmacia
photo foto
photocopy fotocopia
pick-pocket borsaiolo
picnic picnic
piece pezzo
pig maiale
pill pillola
pillow cuscino
pin spilla
pink rosa
pity, it's a che peccato
pizza pizza
plane aereoplano
plain semplice

plant pianta
plastic plastica
plastic bag sacchetto di plastica
plate piatto
platform (train) binario
play (v) giocare
play teatro
please per favore
pliers pinzette
pocket tasca
point (v) indicare
police polizia
poor povero
pork porco
possible possibile
postcard cartolina
poster poster
practical pratico[a]
pregnant incinta
prescription prescrizione
present (gift) regalo
pretty carino[a]
price prezzo
priest prete
private privato
problem problema
profession professione
prohibited proibito
pronunciation pronuncia
public pubblico
pull tirare
purple viola
purse borsa

DICTIONARY

push spingere

Q

quality qualità
quarter (¼) quarto
queen regina
question (n) domanda
quiet tranquillo

R

R.V. camper
rabbit coniglio
radio radio
raft gommone
railway rotaie
rain (n) pioggia
rainbow arcobaleno
raincoat impermeabile
rape (n) violenza carnale
raw crudo
razor rasoio
ready pronto
receipt ricevuta
receive ricevere
receptionist centralinista
recipe ricetta
recommend raccomandare
red rosso
refill (v) riempire
refund (n) rimborso
relax (v) riposare

religion religione
remember ricordare
rent (v) affittare
repair (v) riparare
reserve prenotare
reservation prenotazione
return ritornare
rich ricco[a]
right destra
ring (n) anello
ripe maturo
river fiume
rock (n) pietra
roller skates pattini a rotelle
romantic romantico[a]
roof tetto
room camera
rope corda
rotten marcio
round trip ritorno
rowboat barca a remi
rucksack zaino
rug tappeto
ruins rovine
run (v) correre

S

sad triste
safe sicuro
safety pin spilla da balia
sailing vela
sale liquidazione

same stesso
sandals sandali
sandwich panino
sanitary napkins assorbenti igienici
Saturday sabato
scandalous scandaloso
scarf sciarpa
school scuola
science scienza
scientist scienziato[a]
scissors forbici
scotch tape nastro adesivo
screwdriver cacciaviti
sculptor scultore
sculpture scultura
sea mare
seafood frutti di mare
seat posto
second class secondo classe
secret segreto
see vedere
self-service self-service
sell vendere
send spedire
separate (adj) separato
serious serio
service servizio
sex sesso
sexy sexy
shampoo shampoo
shaving cream crema da barba
she lei

sheet lenzuolo
shell conchiglia
ship (n) nave
shirt camicia
shoes scarpe
shopping fare spese
short corto[a]
shorts pantaloncini
shoulder spalle
show (v) mostrare
show (n) spettacolo
shower doccia
shy timido[a]
sick malato[a]
sign segno
signature firma
silence silenzio
silk seta
silver argento
similar simile
simple semplice
sing cantare
singer cantante
single (m / f) scapolo / nubile
sink lavandino
sir signore
sister sorella
size taglia
skating pattinaggio
ski (v) sciare
skin pelle
skinny magro[a]
skirt gonna

sky cielo
sleep (v) dormire
sleepy assonnato[a]
slice fettina
slide (photo) diapositiva
slippery scivoloso
slow lento
small piccolo[a]
smell (n) odore
smile (n) sorriso
smoking fumare
snack merendina
sneeze (n) starnuto
snore russare
soap sapone
soccer calcio
socks calzini
something qualcosa
son figlio
song canzone
soon subito
sorry mi dispiace
sour acerbo
south sud
speak parlare
specialty specialità
speed velocità
spend spendere
spider ragno
spoon cucchiaio
sport sport
spring primavera
square piazza

stapler pinzatrice
stairs scale
stamps francobolli
star (in sky) stella
state stato
station stazione
stomach stomaco
stop (n) stop / alt
stop (v) fermare
storm temporale
story (floor) storia
straight dritto
strange (odd) strano[a]
stream (n) corrente
street strada
strike (stop work) sciopero
string filo
strong forte
stuck incastrato
student studente
stupid stupido[a]
sturdy resistente
style stile
suddenly improvvisamente
suitcase valigia
summer estate
sun sole
sunbathe abbronzarsi
sunburn bruciatura del sole
Sunday domenica
sunglasses occhiali da sole
sunny assolato
sunset tramonto

sunscreen protezione solare
sunshine sole
sunstroke insolazione
suntan (n) abbronzatura
suntan lotion crema per il sole
supermarket supermercato
supplement supplemento
surprise (n) sorpresa
swallow (v) ingoiare
sweat (v) sudare
sweater maglione
sweet dolce
swim nuotare
swimming pool piscina
swim suit costume da bagno
swim trunks costume de bagno
Switzerland Svizzera
synthetic sintetico

T

table tavolo
tail coda
take prendere
take out (food) portar via
talcum powder borotalco
talk parlare
tall alto
tampons assorbenti interni
tape (cassette) cassetta
taste (n) gusto
taste (v) assaggiare
tax tasse

teacher insegnante
team squadra
teenager adolescente
telephone telefono
television televisione
temperature temperatura
tender tenero
tennis tennis
tennis shoes scarpe da tennis
tent tenda
tent pegs picchetti della tenda
terrible terribile
thanks grazie
theater teatro
thermometer termometro
thick spesso
thief ladro
thigh coscia
thin sottile
thing cosa
think pensare
thirsty assetato
thongs sandali infradito
thread filo
throat gola
through attraverso
throw tirare
Thursday giovedì
ticket biglietto
tight stretto
timetable orario
tired stanco
tissues fazzolettini

to a
today oggi
toe dito del piede
together insieme
toilet toilette
toilet paper carta igienica
tomorrow domani
tonight stanotte
too troppo
tooth dente
toothbrush spazzolino da denti
toothpaste dentifricio
toothpick stuzzicadenti
total totale
tour giro
tourist turista
towel asciugamano
tower torre
town città
toy giocattolo
track (train) binario
traditional tradizionale
traffic traffico
train treno
translate tradurre
travel viaggiare
travel agency agenzia di viaggi
traveler's check traveler's check
tree albero
trip viaggio
trouble guaio
T-shirt maglietta
Tuesday martedì

tunnel tunnel
tweezers pinzette
twins gemelli

U

ugly brutto[a]
umbrella ombrello
uncle zio
under sotto
underpants mutandine
understand capire
underwear mutande
unemployed disoccupato[a]
unfortunately sfortunatamente
United States Stati Uniti
university università
up su
upstairs di sopra
urgent urgente
us noi
use usare

V

vacancy (hotel) camare libere
vacant libero
valley valle
vegetarian (n) vegetariano[a]
very molto
vest panciotto
video video
video camera video camera

video recorder   video registratore
view   vista
village   villaggio
vineyard   vigneto
virus   virus
visit (n)   visita
visit (v)   visitare
vitamins   vitamine
voice   voce
vomit (v)   vomitare

W

waist   vita
wait   aspettare
waiter   cameriere
waitress   cameriera
wake up   svegliarsi
walk (v)   camminare
wallet   portafoglio
want   volere
warm (adj)   caldo
wash   lavare
watch (v)   guardare
watch (n)   orologio
water   acqua
water, tap   acqua del rubinetto
waterfall   cascata
we   noi
weather   tempo
weather forecast   previsioni del tempo
wedding   matrimonio

Wednesday   mercoledì
week   settimana
weight   peso
welcome   benvenuto
west   ovest
wet   bagnato
what   che cosa
wheel   ruota
when   quando
where   dove
whipped cream   panna
white   bianco
white-out   bianchetto
who   chi
why   perchè
widow   vedova
widower   vedovo
wife   moglie
wild   selvaggio[a]
wind   vento
window   finestra
wine   vino
wing   ala
winter   inverno
wish (v)   desiderare
with   con
without   senza
women   donne
wood   legno
wool   lana
word   parola
work (n)   lavoro
work (v)   lavorare

DICTIONARY

world mondo
worse peggio
worst peggiore
wrap incartare
wrist polso
write scrivere

Y

year anno
yellow giallo
yes si
yesterday ieri

you (formal) Lei
you (informal) tu
young giovane
youth hostel ostello della gioventù

Z

zero zero
zip-lock bag busta de plastica sigillabile
zipper chiusura lampo
zoo zoo

Hurdling the Language Barrier

Don't be afraid to communicate

Even the best phrase book won't satisfy your needs in every situation. To really hurdle the language barrier, you need to leap beyond the printed page, and dive into contact with the locals. Never, never, never allow your lack of foreign language skills to isolate you from the people and cultures you traveled halfway 'round the world to experience. Remember that in every country you visit, you're surrounded by expert, native-speaking tutors. Spend bus and train rides letting them teach you.

Always start a conversation by asking politely in the local language, "Do you speak English?" When you communicate in English with someone from another country, speak slowly, clearly, and with carefully chosen words. Use what the Voice of America calls "simple English." You're talking to people who are wishing it was written down, hoping to see each letter as it tumbles out of your mouth. Pronounce each letter, avoiding all contractions and slang. For bad examples, listen to other tourists.

Keep things caveman-simple. Make single nouns work as entire sentences ("Photo?"). Use internationally understood words ("auto kaput" works in Sicily). Butcher the language if you must. The important thing is to make the effort. To get air mail stamps, you can flap your wings and say "tweet, tweet." If you want milk, moo and pull two imaginary udders. Risk looking like a fool.

APPENDIX

If you're short on words, make your picnic a potluck. Pull out a map and point out your journey. Draw what you mean. Bring photos from home and introduce your family. Play cards or toss a Frisbee. Fold an origami bird for kids or dazzle 'em with sleight-of-hand magic.

Go ahead and make educated guesses. Many situations are easy-to-fake multiple choice questions. Practice. Read timetables, concert posters and newspaper headlines. Listen to each language on a multilingual tour. Be melodramatic. Exaggerate the local accent. Self-consciousness is the deadliest communication-killer.

Choose multilingual people to communicate with, such as students, business people, urbanites, young well-dressed people, or anyone in the tourist trade. Use a small note pad to keep track of handy phrases you pick up—and to help you communicate more clearly with the locals by scribbling down numbers, maps, and so on. Some travelers carry important messages written on a small card (vegetarian, boiled water, your finest ice cream).

Easy cultural bugaboos to avoid

■ When writing numbers, give your sevens a cross (7) and give your ones an upswing (1).

■ European dates are different: Christmas is 25-12-96, not 12-25-96.

■ Commas are decimal points and decimals are commas, so a dollar and a half is 1,50 and there are 5.280 feet in a mile.

■ The Italian "first floor" is not the ground floor, but the first floor up.

■ When counting with your fingers, start with your thumb. If you hold up only your first finger, you'll probably get two of something.

Italian tongue twisters (Scioglilingua)

Tongue twisters are a great way to practice a language—and break the ice with the locals. Here are a few that are sure to challenge you, and amuse your hosts:

Trentatrè trentini arrivarono a Trento tutti e trentatrè trottorellando.	Thirty-three people from Trent arrived in Trent, all thirty-three trotting.
Chi fù quel barbaro barbiere che barberò così barbaramente a Piazza Barberini quel povero barbaro di Barbarossa?	Who was that barbarian barber in Barberini Square who shaved that poor barbarian Barbarossa?
Sopra la panca la capra canta, sotto la panca la capra crepa.	On the bench the goat sings, under the bench the goat dies.
Tigre contro tigre.	Tiger against tiger.

APPENDIX

English tongue twisters:

After your Italian friends have laughed at you, let them try these tongue twisters in English:

If neither he sells seashells, nor she sells seashells, who shall sell seashells? Shall seashells be sold?	Se ne' lui vende conchiglie, Ne' lei vende conchiglie, Chi venderà conchiglie, Si venderanno conchiglie?
Peter Piper picked a peck of pickled peppers.	Peter Piper raccolse un mucchio di peperoni sott'aceto.
Rugged rubber baby buggy bumpers.	Imbottitura grezza di gomma di passeggino per bambino.
The sixth sick sheik's sixth sheep's sick.	La sesta pecora del sesto sceicco ammalato è malata.
Red bug's blood and black bug's blood.	Sangue di insetto rosso e sangue di insetto nero.
Soldiers' shoulders.	Spalle da soldato.
Thieves seize skis.	Ladri rubano sci.
I'm a pleasant mother pheasant plucker. I pluck mother pheasants. I'm the most pleasant mother pheasant plucker that ever plucked a mother pheasant.	Sono un piacevole raccoglitore di fagiane madri. Raccolgo fagiane madri. Sono il più piacevole raccoglitore di fagiane madri che abbia mai raccolto fagiane madri.

International words

As our world shrinks, more and more words hop across their linguistic boundaries and become international. Savvy travelers develop a knack for choosing words most likely to be universally understood ("auto" instead of "car," "kaput" rather than "broken," "photo," not "picture"). Internationalize your pronunciation. "University," if you play around with its sound (oo-nee-vehr-see-tay) will be understood anywhere. Practice speaking English with a heavy Italian accent. Wave your arms a lot. Be creative.

Here are a few internationally understood words. Remember, cut out the Yankee accent and give each word a pan-European sound.

Stop	Kaput	Vino	Restaurant
Ciao	Bank	Hotel	Bye-bye
Rock 'n roll	Post	Camping	OK
Auto	Picnic	Amigo	Autobus (boos)
Nuclear	Macho	Tourist	English (Engleesh)
Yankee	Americano	Mama mia	Michelangelo
Beer	Oo la la	Coffee	Casanova (romantic)
Chocolate	Moment	Sexy	Disneyland
Tea	Coca-Cola	No problem	Mañana
Telephone	Photo	Photocopy	Passport
Europa	Self-service	Toilet	Police
Super	Taxi	Central	Information
Pardon	University	Fascist	Rambo
American profanity			

Italian Gestures

Gestures say a lot

In your travels, gestures can either raise or lower the language barrier. For instance, pointing to your head can mean smart in one country and crazy in another. And if you shake your head "no" in Bulgaria, you've just said "yes." Gesture boundaries often follow linguistic ones, but not always. Occasionally a gesture which is very popular in one town or region is meaningless or has a completely different meaning a few miles away.

Here are a few common Italian gestures, their meaning and where you're likely to see them:

The Hand Purse: Straighten the fingers and thumb of one hand, bringing them all together to make an upward point. Your hand can be held still or moved a little up and down at the wrist. This is a common and very Italian gesture for query. It is used to say "What do you want?" or "What are you doing?" or "What is it?" or "What's new?" It can also be used as an insult to say "You fool!"

The Cheek Screw: Make a fist, stick out your forefinger and screw it into your cheek. The cheek screw is used widely and almost exclusively in Italy to mean good, lovely, beautiful. Many Italians also use it to mean clever.

The Eyelid Pull: Place your extended forefinger below the center of your eye, and pull the skin downward. This is a friendly warning, meaning "Be alert, that guy is clever."

The Chin Flick: Tilt your head back slightly, and flick the back of your fingers forward in an arc from under your chin. This means "I don't care, I'm not interested." In southern Italy it can mean "No."

The Forearm Jerk: Clench your right fist, and jerk your forearm up as you slap your bicep with your left palm. This is a rude phallic gesture that men throughout southern Europe use the way Americans give someone "the finger." This extra-large version says "I'm superior" (it's an action some monkeys actually do with their penis to insult their peers).

Tell me what you think.
Your feedback will do a lot to improve future editions of this phrase book. To help tomorrow's travelers travel smarter, please jot down any ideas, phrases, and suggestions as they hit you during your travels, and then send them to me. Mille grazie!

Rick Steves
Europe Through the Back Door
120 Fourth Ave. N, PO Box 2009
Edmonds, WA 98020

APPENDIX

Let's Talk Telephones

Using Italephones

Smart travelers use the telephone every day. Making a hotel reservation by phone the morning of the day you plan to arrive is a snap. If there's a language problem, ask someone at your hotel to talk to your next hotel for you.

The key to long distance is understanding area codes and having an Italian phone card. Hotel room phones are reasonable for local calls, but a terrible rip-off for long-distance calls. Never call home from your hotel room (unless you are putting the call on your calling card).

For calls to other European countries, dial the international access code (00 in Italy), followed by the country code of the country you're calling, followed by the area code without its zero, and finally the local number (four to seven digits). When dialing long distance within Italy, start with the area code (including its zero), then the local number. Post offices have fair, metered long distance booths.

Italian telephone cards are much easier to use than coins for local and long distance calls. Buy one on your first day to force you to find smart reasons to use the local phones. The 5000 or 10,000 lire cards are worth from $3 to $7. You can buy them at post offices, *tabacchi* shops, and machines near phone booths (many phone booths indicate where the nearest phone card sales outlet is located). The old vandal-plagued coin- and token-operated phones work if you have the necessary pile of coins.

Dial patiently in Italy, as if the phone doesn't understand numbers very well. Sometimes you'll need to try again and again. When you finally get through, don't hesitate to nearly scream to be heard.

Calling the USA from a pay phone is easy if you have an Italian phone card, or an ATT, MCI or SPRINT calling card. Or you can call using coins ($1 for 15 seconds) and ask the other person to call you back at your hotel at a specified time. Italy-to-USA calls are twice as expensive as direct calls from the States. Midnight in California is breakfast in Rome. To call the USA from Italy, dial 00-1-area code-local number. To call Italy from the USA, dial 011-39-Italian area code (without the zero)-local number.

If you plan to call home often, get an ATT, MCI or SPRINT card. You don't actually put the card in the phone; you give the card number to an American operator. Each card company has a toll-free number in each European country which puts you in touch with an American operator who takes your card number and the number you want to call, puts you through, and bills your home phone number for the call (at the cheaper USA rate of about a dollar a minute plus a $2.50 service charge). If you talk for at least 3 minutes, you'll save enough to make up for the service charge.

ATT, MCI, & SPRINT operators in Italy:

ATT:	172-1011
MCI:	172-1022
SPRINT:	172-1877

APPENDIX

Country telephone codes:

Austria:	43	Germany:	49	Portugal:	351
Belgium:	32	Greece:	30	Spain:	34
Britain:	44	Hungary:	36	Sweden:	46
Czech Rep.:	42	Ireland:	353	Switzerland:	41
Denmark:	45	Netherlands:	31	Turkey:	90
France:	33	Norway:	47	USA/Canada:	1

Weather

First line is average daily low (°F.); second line average daily high (°F.); third line, days of no rain.

	J	F	M	A	M	J	J	A	S	O	N	D
Rome	39	39	42	46	55	60	64	64	61	53	46	41
	54	56	62	68	74	82	88	88	83	73	63	56
	23	17	26	24	25	28	29	28	24	22	22	22

Metric conversions (approximate)

1 inch = 25 millimeters   1 foot = .3 meter

1 yard = .9 meter   1 mile = 1.6 kilometers

1 sq. yard = .8 sq. meter   1 acre = 0.4 hectare

1 quart = .95 liter   1 ounce = 28 grams

1 pound = .45 kilo   1 kilo = 2.2 pounds

1 centimeter = 0.4 inch   1 meter = 39.4 inches

1 kilometer = .62 mile

Miles = kilometers divided by 2 plus 10%

(120 km ÷ 2 = 60, 60 + 12 = 72 miles)

Fahrenheit degrees = double Celsius + 30

32° F = 0° C, 82° F = about 28° C

Your tear-out cheat sheet

Keep this sheet of the most essential Italian words and phrases in your pocket, so you can memorize them during idle moments, or quickly refer to them if you're caught without your phrase book.

Good day.	Buon giorno.	bwohn **jor**-noh
Do you speak English?	Parla inglese?	**par**-lah een-**glay**-zay
Yes. / No.	Sì. / No.	see / noh
I don't speak Italian.	Non parlo l'italiano.	nohn **par**-loh lee-tah-leeah-noh
I'm sorry.	Mi dispiace.	mee dee-speeah-chay
Please.	Per favore.	pehr fah-**voh**-ray
Thank you.	Grazie.	**graht**-seeay
It's (not) a problem.	(Non) c'è problema.	(nohn) cheh proh-**blay**-mah
It's good.	Va bene.	vah **behn**-ay
You are very kind.	Lei è molto gentile.	lehee eh **mohl**-toh jayn-**tee**-lay
Goodbye!	Arrivederci!	ah-ree-vay-**dehr**-chee
Where is...?	Dov'è...?	doh-**veh**
...a hotel	...un hotel	oon oh-**tehl**
...a youth hostel	...un ostello della gioventù	oon oh-**stehl**-loh **day**-lah joh-vehn-**too**
...a restaurant	...un ristorante	oon ree-stoh-**rahn**-tay
...a supermarket	...un supermercado	oon soo-pehr-mehr-**kah**-doh
...a pharmacy	...una farmacia	**oo**-nah far-mah-**chee**-ah
...a bank	...una banca	**oo**-nah **bahn**-kah
...the train station	...la stazione	lah staht-seeoh-nay
...tourist information	...informazioni per turisti	een-for-maht-seeoh-nee pehr too-**ree**-stee
...the toilet	...la toilette	lah twah-**leht**-tay
men	uomini, signori	**woh**-mee-nee, seen-**yoh**-ree
women	donne, signore	**don**-nay, seen-**yoh**-ray

How much is it?	**Quanto costa?**	kwahn-toh **kos**-tah
Write it?	**Lo scrive?**	loh **skree**-vay
Cheap(er).	**(Più) economico.**	(pew) ay-koh-**noh**-mee-koh
Cheapest.	**Il più economico.**	eel pew ay-koh-**noh**-mee-koh
Is it free?	**È gratis?**	eh **grah**-tees
Is it included?	**È incluso?**	eh een-**kloo**-zoh
Do you have...?	**Ha...?**	ah
I would like...	**Vorrei....**	vor-**rehee**
We would like...	**Vorremo...**	vor-**ray**-moh
...this.	**...questo.**	**kway**-stoh
...just a little.	**...un pochino.**	oon poh-**kee**-noh
...more.	**...di più.**	dee pew
...a ticket.	**...un biglietto.**	oon beel-**yay**-toh
...a room.	**...una camera.**	**oo**-nah **kah**-may-rah
...the bill.	**...il conto.**	eel **kohn**-toh
one	**uno**	**oo**-noh
two	**due**	**doo**-ay
three	**tre**	tray
four	**quattro**	**kwah**-troh
five	**cinque**	**cheeng**-kway
six	**sei**	**seh**ee
seven	**sette**	**seht**-tay
eight	**otto**	**ot**-toh
nine	**nove**	**nov**-ay
ten	**dieci**	**deeay**-chee
hundred	**cento**	**chehn**-toh
thousand	**mille**	**mee**-lay
At what time?	**A che ora?**	ah kay **oh**-rah
Just a moment.	**Un momento.**	oon moh-**mayn**-toh
Now.	**Adesso.**	ah-**dehs**-soh
soon / later	**presto / tardi**	**prehs**-toh / **tar**-dee
today / tomorrow	**oggi / domani**	**oh**-jee / doh-**mah**-nee

Rick Steves' Europe Through the Back Door Catalog

All of these items have been especially designed for independent budget travelers. They have been thoroughly field tested by Rick Steves and his globe-trotting ETBD staff, and are completely guaranteed. Prices include shipping, tax, and a free subscription to Rick's quarterly newsletter/catalog.

Back Door Bag convertible suitcase/backpack $75

At 9"x21"x13" this specially-designed, sturdy, functional bag is maximum carry-on-the-plane size (fits under the seat), and your key to foot-loose and fancy-free travel. Made in the USA from rugged, water-resistant 1000 denier Cordura nylon, it converts from a smart-looking suitcase to a handy backpack. It has hide-away padded shoulder straps, top and side handles, and a detachable shoulder strap (for toting as a suitcase). Beefy, lockable perimeter zippers allow easy access to the roomy (2500 cubic inches) main compartment. Two large outside pockets are perfect for frequently used items. A nylon stuff bag is also included. Over 50,000 Back Door travelers have used these bags around the world. Rick Steves helped design this bag, and lives out of it for 3 months at a time. Comparable bags cost much more. Available in black, grey, navy blue and très chic teal green.

European railpasses

...cost the same everywhere, but only ETBD gives you a free hour-long "How to get the most out of your railpass" video, free advice on your itinerary, and your choice of one of Rick Steves' regional "Best of..." guidebooks. For starters, call 206/771-8303, and we'll send you a free copy of Rick Steves' Annual Guide to European Railpasses.

Moneybelt $8

Absolutely required no matter where you're traveling! An ultra-light, sturdy, under-the-pants, one-size-fits-all nylon pouch, our svelte moneybelt is just the right size to carry your passport, airline tickets and traveler's checks comfortably. Made to ETBD's exacting specifications, this moneybelt is your best defense against theft—when you wear it, feeling a street urchin's hand in your pocket becomes just another interesting cultural experience.

Prices include shipping within the USA/Canada, and are good through 1995—maybe longer. Orders will be processed within 2 weeks. For rush orders (which we process within 48 hours), please add $10. Washington residents please add 8.2% sales tax. Send your check to:

Rick Steves' Europe Through the Back Door
120 Fourth Ave. N, PO Box 2009
Edmonds, WA 98020

More books by Rick Steves...

*Now more than ever, travelers are determined to get the most out of every mile, minute and dollar. That's what Rick's books are all about. He'll help you have a better trip **because** you're on a budget, not in spite of it. Each of these books is published by John Muir Publications, and is available through your local bookstore, or through Rick's free Europe Through the Back Door newsletter/catalog.*

Rick Steves' Europe Through The Back Door

Updated every year, *ETBD* has given thousands of people the skills and confidence they needed to travel through the less-touristed "back doors" of Europe. You'll find chapters on packing, itinerary-planning, transportation, finding rooms, travel photography, keeping safe and healthy, plus chapters on Rick's favorite back door discoveries.

Mona Winks: Self-Guided Tours of Europe's Top Museums

Let's face it, museums can ruin a good vacation. But *Mona* takes you by the hand, giving you fun and easy-to-follow self-guided tours through Europe's 20 most frightening and exhausting museums and cultural obligations. Packed with more than 200 maps and illustrations.

Europe 101: History and Art for the Traveler

A lively, entertaining crash course in European history and art, *Europe 101* is the perfect way to prepare yourself for the rich cultural smorgasbord that awaits you.

Rick Steves' Best of Europe
Rick Steves' Best of Great Britain
Rick Steves' Best of France, Belgium & the Netherlands
Rick Steves' Best of Italy
Rick Steves' Best of Germany, Austria & Switzerland
Rick Steves' Best of Scandinavia
Rick Steves' Best of Spain & Portugal
Rick Steves' Best of the Baltics & Russia

For a successful trip, raw information isn't enough. In his *Best of...* guides, Rick Steves weeds through the endless possibilities each region offers, to give you candid, straightforward advice on what to see, where to sleep, how to manage your time, and how to get the most out of every dollar. Rick personally updates these guides every year.

Rick Steves' European Phrase Books: French, Italian, German, Spanish/Portuguese, and French/Italian/German

Finally, a series of phrase books written especially for the budget traveler! Each book gives you the words and phrases you need to communicate with the locals about room-finding, transportation, food, health—you'll even learn how to start conversations about politics, philosophy and romance—all spiced with Rick Steves' travel tips, and his unique blend of down-to-earth practicality and humor. All are 1995 editions.

What we do at Europe Through the Back Door

At ETBD we value travel as a powerful way to better understand and contribute to the world in which we live. Our mission at ETBD is to equip travelers with the confidence and skills necessary to travel through Europe independently, economically, and in a way that is culturally broadening. To accomplish this, we:

■ Teach budget European travel skills seminars (often for free);

■ Research and write guidebooks to Europe;

■ Write and host a Public Television series;

■ Sell European railpasses, our favorite guidebooks, maps, travel bags, and other travel accessories;

■ Provide European travel consulting services;

■ Organize and lead lively Back Door tours of Europe, France, Italy, Turkey, and beyond;

■ Run a Travel Resource Center in espresso-correct Edmonds, WA;

...and we travel a lot.

Back Door 'Best of Europe' tours

If you like our independent travel philosophy but would like to benefit from the camaraderie and efficiency of group travel, our Back Door tours may be right up your alley. Every year we lead friendly, intimate 'Best of Europe in 22 Days' tours, free-spirited 'Bus, Bed & Breakfast' tours, and special regional tours of Turkey, Britain, France, and other fun places. For details, call 206/771-8303 and ask for our free newsletter/catalog.

Faxing your hotel reservation

Most hotel managers know basic "hotel English." Use this handy form for your fax.

. . . .

One page fax   My fax #:_____

To: Today's date: ____ / ____ / ____

From: day   month   year

Dear Hotel _____,
    Please make this reservation for me:

Name: _____

Total # of people: ____   # of rooms: ____   # of nights: ____

Arriving: ____ / ____ / ____   Time of arrival (24-hour clock): _____

           day   month   year   (I will telephone if later)

Departing: ____ / ____ / ____

             day   month   year

Room(s):   Single   Double   Twin   Triple   Quad   Quint

With: Toilet   Shower   Bath   Sink only

Special needs: View   Quiet   Cheapest room   Ground floor

Credit card: Visa   Mastercard   American Express

Card #: _____   Exp. date: _____

Name on card: _____

If a deposit is necessary, you may charge me for the first night. Please fax or mail me confirmation of my reservation, the type of room reserved, the price, and if the price includes breakfast. Thank you.

Signed: _____   Phone: _____

Address: _____

Other Books from John Muir Publications

Travel Books by Rick Steves
Asia Through the Back Door,
4th ed., 400 pp. $16.95
Europe 101: History, Art, and
Culture for the Traveler,
4th ed., 372 pp. $15.95
Mona Winks: Self-Guided Tours
of Europe's Top Museums,
2nd ed., 456 pp. $16.95
Rick Steves' Best of the Baltics
and Russia, 1995 ed. 144 pp.
$9.95
Rick Steves' Best of Europe,
1995 ed., 544 pp. $16.95
Rick Steves' Best of France,
Belgium, and the Netherlands,
1995 ed., 240 pp. $12.95
Rick Steves' Best of Germany,
Austria, and Switzerland, 1995
ed., 240 pp. $12.95
Rick Steves' Best of Great
Britain, 1995 ed., 192 pp.
$11.95
Rick Steves' Best of Italy, 1995
ed., 208 pp. $11.95
Rick Steves' Best of
Scandinavia, 1995 ed.,
192 pp. $11.95

Rick Steves' Best of Spain and
Portugal, 1995 ed., 192 pp.
$11.95
Rick Steves' Europe Through
the Back Door, 13th ed.,
480 pp. $17.95
Rick Steves' French Phrase
Book, 2nd ed., 112 pp. $4.95
Rick Steves' German Phrase
Book, 2nd ed., 112 pp. $4.95
Rick Steves' Italian Phrase
Book, 2nd ed., 112 pp. $4.95
Rick Steves' Spanish and
Portuguese Phrase Book, 2nd
ed., 288 pp. $5.95
Rick Steves' French/German/
Italian Phrase Book, 288 pp.
$6.95

European Travel Titles For
Young Readers
Ages 8 & Up
Kidding Around London,
2nd ed., 64 pp., $9.95
Kidding Around Paris,
2nd ed., 64 pp., $9.95
Kidding Around Spain,
108 pp. $12.95